One Woman's Commitment to the Children of Nepal

Olga Murray with Mary Sutro Callender

First Edition
Copyright © 2015 by Olga Murray

All rights reserved, including the right of reproduction in whole or in part in any form.

ISBN-13: 978-1512269345
ISBN-10: 1512269344

Published by
Olga Murray Publications

Cover and book design by Todd Towner
Cover photograph of Olga and two children
by Cherilyn Parsons
Printed in the United States of America

This book is dedicated to the wonderful children of Nepal, with gratitude for all the love, all the joy, all the fun we have shared.

Each time a man stands up for an ideal, or acts to improve the lot of others, or strikes out against injustice, he sends forth a tiny ripple of hope, and crossing each other from a million different centers of energy and daring, those ripples build a current that can sweep down the mightiest walls of oppression and resistance.

— Robert F. Kennedy

Nepal is a land-locked nation, squeezed between China on the north and India on the south. Among the poorest and least developed countries on earth, it is about the size of Arkansas, with a population of thirty million people. The land slopes from the mighty snow-capped Himalayas to the flat, steamy, level plains and jungles along the Indian border, known as the Terai.

Over seventy-five percent of Nepalis live in rural areas, where the main occupation is farming. Kathmandu, the capital, is by far the largest city, with a population of over one million people.

Although the official language is Nepali, there are one hundred twenty-five caste or ethnic groups, speaking almost as many languages. Eighty-one percent of the population is Hindu. More than half of Nepalese are under twenty-four years of age and there are about 2.4 million child laborers between five to fourteen years old.

CONTENTS

Foreword by Arzu Deuba		1
Preface		3
Chapter 1	Daughters for Sale	5
Chapter 2	A Piglet for a Girl	15
Chapter 3	Olga's Promise	27
Chapter 4	Little Girl from the Bronx	43
Chapter 5	Finding My Way	55
Chapter 6	Settling Down: Marriage and Career	63
Chapter 7	Children of a Lesser God	79
Chapter 8	New Beginnings	95
Chapter 9	Family Life	107
Chapter 10	Changes and Challenges	125
Chapter 11	Combating the Scourge of Malnutrition	139
Chapter 12	Ancient Roots of Injustice	151
Chapter 13	Girl Power	169
Chapter 14	Free, Free at Last!	177
Afterword		187
Postscript: The 2015 Earthquake in Nepal		193
Acknowledgments		205
Join the Nepal Youth Foundation Family		209
About the Authors		210

FOREWORD

Our life on this Earth is finite, thus every second counts. Though none of us can determine when we come and when we will go, we are masters of what we choose to do while we are here. Olga Murray is one of those rare beings who puts a real value on the preciousness of our short time on Earth.

The first time I saw Olga, I thought she had stepped out of one of my favorite childhood tales—she looked just as I imagined the Good Fairy would look. Her reputation for good works preceded my first meeting with her fifteen years ago, so maybe that had already put a halo on her head for me. But unlike many instances in life where the first meeting leaves a good impression but the rest is all downhill, every meeting with Olga got better over the years.

Olga's quest for rescuing Nepali children and seeing them through until they are settled on their way towards a good life is commendable, as well as inspirational. Especially when you think of the fact that she came from the other end of the world and started the Nepal Youth Foundation after she retired from her career as a lawyer. This type of energy can only come from a deep commitment and love for others. Olga is one of the youngest persons I have known in my life. Her energy level and zest for life are exceptional. Every time I meet her, I come away feeling a bit younger.

In my opinion, Olga's work for the bonded Kamlari girls of Nepal is worth an international human rights award. She has worked tirelessly through the Nepal Youth Foundation to rescue girls from slavery and offer them alternatives for a better, more dignified life. I have met some of the girls rescued by Olga and am so impressed to see the confidence they have in their future. I find it amazing, especially when I realize the alternatives they would have faced if a Good Fairy named Olga had not touched their lives.

I wish to thank Olga for the love and dedication she has given to all the Nepali children whose lives she has changed for the better. I feel truly blessed to have met her.

Dr. Arzu Rana Deuba is a member of the Constituent Assembly of Nepal. A passionate advocate for women's rights, she founded the Safe Motherhood Network Federation of Nepal, the Rural Women's Development and Unity Centre and Saathi, an organization that combats domestic violence. In addition, Dr. Deuba serves as a board member and consultant for numerous environmental, educational and social service organizations. She is married to Sher Bahadur Deuba, the former Prime Minister of Nepal.

PREFACE

Some women fall in love with men—I fall in love with countries. In 1984, approaching the age of retirement as a research attorney at the California Supreme Court, I visited Nepal to go trekking in the Himalayas. Totally unexpectedly, I discovered a country and a cause to which I would devote the rest of my life.

During the trek from Pokhara to Siklis, we walked through remote villages where children lived in abject poverty. The stunningly beautiful surroundings and the friendliness of the people overwhelmed me. But beyond that, it was the children I encountered who made the deepest impression of all. They were poor beyond anything I had ever experienced—dirty, dressed in ragged clothes, malnourished, without toys of any sort. And yet, they were the most joyful, funny, amiable little kids anywhere on earth. Their most fervent wish was to go to school someday.

I was almost 60, and perhaps subconsciously, I was searching for something worthwhile to do following my retirement. After returning to my sleeping bag one night, in a flash, I knew for certain what it was —somehow, I would find a way to educate Nepali children. American dollars go a long way in Nepal, and I realized that for the price of a good haircut back in the States, I could make a significant difference in a child's life in Nepal. This book, written 30 years later, is the story of how I realized, and even surpassed, that dream.

Olga

CHAPTER ONE

DAUGHTERS FOR SALE

The roar of the motorcycle startled her. Then she saw the man. On a bitterly cold day in January 1996, Urmila was huddled by the fire pit with her mother and older brother, Amar. She was six years old. She watched the stranger pull up beside her family's little hut and approach them. He was wearing a shiny suit and tie, and dark sunglasses. She had never seen such clothing, but she knew right away that he had come from the city. She shivered.

He wanted to buy a young girl to work as a domestic servant for a wealthy family in Kathmandu, a large city hundreds of miles away from their village. The man offered Amar 4,000 rupees to buy Urmila's services for a year. He promised Amar that his sister would be educated and well cared for by her employer.

Amar did not hesitate. He owed money to the owner of the farm where his family lived. When their father had fallen ill several months earlier, Amar, the eldest son, became the head of the family. He had borrowed money from the landlord to cover his father's medical expenses and had not been able to repay him. Since then, the landlord had come by almost every day, threatening to evict the family. Four thousand rupees (approximately $70) was a lot of money—more than enough to repay the landlord.

Urmila pleaded with her mother not to send her away, but Amar agreed to the deal. In a desperate bid to escape, Urmila fled. She ran behind a neighbor's hut and hid in the goat shed. Amar followed her. "It is your duty to become a servant so our family will no longer be burdened by debt," he insisted. Her heart sank. She thought it would only last for a year.

It would be four years before she saw her parents again, and 11 years before she was free.

Urmila Chaudhary was born in Manpur, a village in the Dang District of Southwestern Nepal. She and her family of 11 lived in a small bamboo-and-mud hut, with pumpkin vines sprawling across the thatched straw roof. They had no electricity, running water or furniture. Several enormous decorative clay containers for storing rice and grains loomed large in the hut's dark interior. Animals roamed freely throughout the village—chickens and ducks scurried about the yard, pigs wallowed in muddy pits and water buffalo meandered through the fields.

Like most young girls growing up in the Dang District, Urmila was expected to help with daily chores. She accompanied her mother to the landlord's house to help clean, wash dishes and fold laundry. At home, she swept the dirt floor of their little hut, collected wood, fetched water, sifted rice and looked after her young nieces and nephews. Her sisters taught her how to forage in the forest for plants and roots they could boil to feed the family. She learned how to make primitive shoes by tying bean pods to her feet with pieces of rope. Despite long hours of chores, Urmila and her friends in the village had time to play tag, hopscotch, marbles and jump rope.

Some days, Urmila and her grandfather walked through the bright green rice paddies as they led the cattle to graze in the nearby jungle. Along the way, they listened to women singing while they worked in the fields carrying bundles of bright yellow mustard on their heads. They heard the strange call of peacocks and the rustling of tall trees in the jungle.

No one in Urmila's family had ever attended school. Over half the population in the Dang District were illiterate, most of them women. Many families did not have even the few rupees needed to send their children to school. Occasionally, Urmila and her younger brother were allowed to go to evening classes at the village school, where they learned basic numbers and the Nepali alphabet.

Like most of their neighbors, Urmila's family are Tharus, members of an impoverished ethnic community living in the Terai region of Nepal, a predominantly Hindu nation. A belt of grasslands, savannas and dense forests, the Terai is located south of the outer Himalayan foothills close to the Indian border. For centuries, the Tharu people lived communally, cultivating the land in the fertile plains, fishing the rivers and hunting in the nearby forest. They lived in relative isolation and had little contact with the outside world. Malaria was prevalent in the area, but the Tharus had developed resistance to it. Strangers, however, stayed away because of the threat of disease.

With the introduction of DDT-spraying programs throughout the swamps and dense forests in the 1950s, malaria in the Terai was practically eradicated, and a large influx of farmers from the hills descended on the fertile plains in search of arable land. They settled in Dang and the four adjoining districts: Banke, Bardiya, Kailali and Kanchanpur. The newcomers usurped land that had been farmed for centuries by the Tharus, who had no records or deeds to the land and could not afford the property taxes. When the newcomers laid claim to the land by paying taxes and registering it in their own names, many Tharus lost their farms.

They were forced to work as agricultural laborers on land they had formerly owned, cultivating the fields and managing to eke out a minimal existence as sharecroppers. When they needed cash for medical care, clothing, or a special occasion such as a wedding, they had no alternative but to ask the landlord for a loan. The landowners dictated the terms and most of them charged exorbitant interest rates. Unable to repay the loans, the Tharus were soon buried under tremendous debt, which was passed on from father to son. Eventually, entire families were forced into a bonded labor system called kamaiya. The Tharu farmers became virtual slaves.

Before long, the new landowners began demanding that Tharu men send their wives and daughters to work in their homes, expecting them to cook, clean and do laundry. They were forced to comply, rather than risk losing their livelihood. Within a generation, this led to the widespread practice known as kamlari, the bonded slavery of young Tharu girls, who were called by the same name.

As daughters of the wealthy landlords grew up and got married, they left home to live with their new husbands and often took the Kamlaris with them as a dowry. Gradually, the custom of girl-child indentured labor spread beyond the Dang Valley to the four adjoining districts. With an expanding network of roads and the resulting urbanization, city dwellers from as far away as Kathmandu realized they could get cheap labor by buying a Tharu girl to work in their homes. Middlemen began to visit Tharu communities to buy servants for wealthy employers in return for commissions or favors.

The annual festival of Maghe Sankranti marks the end of Poush, a month when all religious ceremonies are forbidden, and coincides with the end of winter and the advent of warmer weather. The Tharu community observes the mid-January festival with much fanfare. Days are filled with feasting, dancing, drinking, singing and cultural performances. Friends, neighbors and families gather to worship at shrines and temples and take ritual cleansing baths in the frigid rivers. Women dress in colorful traditional costumes and young people go door to door throughout the villages to seek blessings from their elders.

But beneath the revelry, a sinister undercurrent of tension and fear ripples through the community. Maghe Sankranti marks the end of the Tharu fiscal year—the time when all debts must be settled. Knowing that many men are desperate for money to repay landlords or other creditors, agents arrive in the villages to negotiate or renew one-year kamlari contracts. During the festival, the buying and selling of Kamlari girls hits a fevered pitch.

Tempted by easy cash, many Tharu fathers agree to sell their daughters into bondage for about $70, the same amount that Urmila's brother was paid. Some, however, receive no money at all, just a few bags of rice or a promise that they could remain on the land. Most are desperately poor, and a girl's wages represent a substantial contribution to the family's meager income. Beyond the cash incentive, middlemen routinely promise parents that their daughters will be well cared for and sent to school. Some families are persuaded that their daughters will have a better life if they work for a wealthy employer who will educate them.

Tharu girls, some as young as six, are sent to private homes, hotels and tea houses throughout Nepal, where they work for powerful politicians, government officials, lawyers, journalists, police officers, and in one case, the employee of an international aid organization. They are forced to work long hours cooking, serving, cleaning, shopping, doing laundry and caring for children barely younger than themselves. Promises to send them to school are rarely honored and opportunities for abuse are rampant. Many girls are beaten or sexually abused. Others simply disappear. Parents are told that their daughter ran away. Some employers offer outrageous explanations. One man told the parents of a Kamlari that their daughter had died from a poisonous snakebite, so he threw her body in the river.

To the credit of the Nepali government, in 2000 it abolished the kamaiya system, which indentured Tharu men. By statute, all debts incurred by kamaiyas to their landlords were forgiven. But the practice of bonding young girls persisted. Even though the government promised to provide land and rehabilitation services to the former kamaiyas, it failed to fulfill this promise in many cases. Desperate for money, more and more Tharu families sent their daughters off to work as indentured servants, leading to an explosion in the number of Kamlaris.

Urmila was sold as a Kamlari during the Maghe celebration in January 1997. As part of the deal, Amar promised to deliver his sister to her new employer. After the festival, Amar and Urmila traveled by bus to Ghorahi, a noisy regional town in southwestern Nepal's Dang District, crowded with honking cars, motorcycles and bicycle rickshaws.

"When I came to the city," Urmila recalls, "I was six years old. My memories from that time are vague. All I remember is crossing the river on my brother's shoulders because I could not do it. When I think of it now, how could a little girl who had to be carried herself work in a stranger's house?"

After Amar dropped Urmila at the home of the wealthy man who had purchased her, she was introduced to his daughter, Sita, who was visiting from Kathmandu with her two children. The man had bought Urmila as a gift for his daughter. "She's too small to do any real work," Sita complained. Her father assured her that Urmila would get used to hard work.

Several days later, Sita departed for Kathmandu with her children and Urmila. During the 260 mile bus ride from Ghorahi, Urmila tried to imagine what the big city would be like. Villagers had told her there were thousands of cars and people everywhere. They said you could buy anything imaginable there—even televisions as big as houses and statues made of gold.

Urmila wondered what her life would be like in the big city. She had overheard women in her village sharing stories about the suffering they had endured as Kamlaris when they were young. Some of them had been forced to sleep on the kitchen floor or under the stairs, they were frequently beaten and ate leftovers scraped from others' plates, a practice considered ritually impure and deeply degrading in Nepal.

Urmila wondered if she would be beaten if she displeased her new mistress. Would her employer keep the promise to send her to school? When would she see her family again?

When the bus arrived in Kathmandu in the evening, the city was buried under a dense layer of smog. Urmila was overwhelmed at the sight of lights coming from every direction and the streets jammed with motorcycles, buses, cars, trucks and people. The bus terminal was a chaotic maelstrom, with men hurling suitcases off the roof of the bus and everyone shouting, using words she didn't understand. Terrified, Urmila clung to Sita so she wouldn't get lost in the crowd.

The villagers had warned Urmila about the bone-chilling cold of winter in Kathmandu, but the weather in the city was worse than anything she could have imagined. Everyone was bundled in jackets, sturdy shoes, hats and gloves; Urmila was wearing only flimsy plastic sandals and light clothing. Her feet became numb, her teeth chattered and smoke seemed to come out of her mouth as she exhaled into the frigid air. She felt desperately homesick, scared and alone.

Once settled in Sita's apartment, Urmila took care of Sita's two children, who were only slightly younger than she was. They ordered her around and treated her as their personal servant—which, of course, she was. "There was no private life, festival or joyful moment for me," Urmila recalls. "I wanted to enjoy and celebrate the festivals, but I had to hide my desire because I was only a servant. Sita's children used to play with motor toys, but all I could do was watch them. I was never allowed to play."

In Nepal, extended families live together, so Urmila was forced to meet relentless demands from a dozen of Sita's relatives. No matter how hard she worked, she could not keep up. Sita was kind to Urmila, but the men in the family often beat her, complaining that her housework was shoddy or punishing her for no reason. Sita's brother-in-law was especially volatile. Once, he slapped Urmila so hard that she fell to the ground. Another time, in a rage, he scalded her arm with boiling water. Each time Sita's brother-in-law abused Urmila, he threatened to beat her again if she dared to tell Sita. The men in the family sent Urmila out to buy cigarettes, but their wives would punish her if she did so; if she refused, the men would beat her. "When things were very bad," Urmila recalled, "I used to think of my mother's hand on my head and the way she took care of me when I had a fever or headache."

Despite the hardship and abuse, Urmila clung to the hope that Sita would send her to school. She wanted to learn how to read and write, and sometimes she sat with the children when they did their homework, peering over their shoulders. Occasionally, one of them handed Urmila a sheet of paper and a pencil and showed her how to write letters and numbers. But if Sita or another relative entered the room, Urmila quickly hid the paper, knowing that she would be punished if she were caught. One evening, the sister-in-law found Urmila reading a book. She lashed out, calling her an ungrateful brat for wasting electricity. "You are just a Kamlari. Reading is not for you," she shouted and snapped off the light.

For many years, whenever Urmila asked her mistress if she could go to school, Sita made excuses. But when Urmila turned 14, Sita finally relented and enrolled her in a government school. Sita's brother-in-law and sister-in-law were furious. They scolded Sita, telling her it was wrong to send a servant to school because she would just get fancy ideas and become rebellious. Taunting Sita, they asked if she would now become the housemaid and do all the cooking and cleaning. When Urmila overheard them yelling at Sita, she was devastated. She knew her dream of going to school was shattered.

As Urmila's workload grew heavier with constant demands from the relatives, she became more exhausted and miserable. Though she liked Sita, she hated her family, especially her arrogant brother-in-law and his deceitful wife. She begged Sita to let her work just for her or send her back to her family in Manpur. After more than eight years, Sita decided to send Urmila to work for her aunt. She assured Urmila that she would have a better life with a room of her own and good pay. Urmila accepted her fate, thinking that her life could not possibly get worse.

She was wrong.

At the age of 14, Urmila moved in with Sita's aunt, a wealthy politician who lived alone in a large house in Kathmandu. The heavy iron gate of the villa was always locked to keep intruders out, but Urmila felt imprisoned inside. She was forbidden to leave the house alone.

Her new employer treated Urmila brutally, forcing her to cook, clean, do laundry and other household chores for 16 to 18 hours a day. If Urmila displeased her mistress, she screamed at her, "You are so stupid! It's no wonder Tharu girls can only work as housemaids." The woman insisted that she be addressed as "Your Excellency," but Urmila secretly thought of her as "Cruel Ma'am."

After almost four miserable years working for Cruel Ma'am, Urmila's life changed dramatically. Cruel Ma'am's son belonged to a local drama group called Gurukul. After a visit with his mother, he left behind a brochure from the theater. Leafing through it, Urmila came across a photograph of several formerly bonded girls staging a play to protest the kamlari custom. She stared at the picture and recognized some girls from her village. She could not believe her eyes. Barely able to read the text, she was able to make out that the article mentioned a group called the Nepal Youth Foundation (NYF) that was rescuing and educating former Kamlaris from the Dang District. Could it be that there were people who actually cared about the fate of Kamlaris? She found a phone number for the foundation in the brochure and called the office several times, but hung up fearfully when someone answered.

What Urmila did not know was that the Nepal Youth Foundation had organized a massive advocacy and awareness campaign against the kamlari practice in the Dang District, including Urmila's village. The foundation's team of local motivators went door to door to convince parents to allow their bonded daughters to come home. During one of these visits, they learned that Urmila had been sold away, and on many occasions they urged her brother to bring her home. Soon after she found the brochure, Urmila convinced Cruel Ma'am to let her return to Manpur for the Maghe festival. Kamlaris were often allowed to go home for a few days to stay with their families during the celebration. Urmila, however, had only been home for the festival twice in 11 years.

When her mistress agreed, Urmila contacted her brother, Amar, and asked him to come to Cruel Ma'am's house to escort her home. As the heavy iron gate of the villa swung shut behind them, Urmila felt a tremendous sense of relief. She was finally returning to Manpur to be reunited with her family and was determined never to return to Cruel Ma'am's house. Her brother insisted there was nothing to go home for—no good place to live, little food and no opportunity to go to school. But Urmila was not discouraged. She told Amar that some people were rescuing and educating the Kamlaris and she hoped to join them and go to school.

"When we reached our village," Urmila recalls, "we saw a group gathering in front of the school. I saw many girls like me there. They told me they were joining a rally organized by the Nepal Youth Foundation to celebrate Kamlari Day, and I said that I also wanted to be part of it because I had spent my life working as a Kamlari. Instead of going home first, I went directly on the rally with them. They were holding signs with slogans such as *Daughters Want Education, Not Slavery*.

"One week later, some people from the foundation came by and counseled me on studying. They gave me a beautiful Tharu dress and told me, 'All we need is your determination. We're here to see to the rest of it.' After that, I felt so relieved and liberated. My hopes to go to school were alive."

CHAPTER TWO

A PIGLET FOR A GIRL

In 1990, when I started the Nepal Youth Foundation to educate Nepali children, I never imagined that child slavery existed in the country. Nine years later, I first heard about the kamlari tradition and was outraged that little girls as young as six years old were sold by their parents to work as domestic servants. Someone had to do something to end this dreadful practice—and maybe that someone was our foundation.

Slavery? In my own country? Not possible, thought Som Paneru, a Nepali who worked as a program assistant for the foundation. It was November 1999. He had just read in the *Kantipur*, a local newspaper, that parents in the Tharu ethnic community would be bonding their daughters away to work as Kamlaris during the upcoming Maghe Sankranti festival in January. Though he had spent his entire life in Nepal, he had never heard of the kamlari practice.

When Som called to tell me what he had learned, I was also shocked and disturbed. We agreed that we needed to find out more. Two days later, Som and a college friend who spoke the Tharu dialect traveled a grueling 13 hours by bus from Kathmandu to the small village of Khaira in the Dang District. They decided to visit Dang first because we had heard that more children were bonded away from there than any other district. It was just a few weeks before the beginning of the Maghe festival.

Som spoke with many parents of young girls who had been sold as domestic servants and they told him similar stories—girls were supposed to work as Kamlaris. To the villagers, this was not shocking at all. The custom had become a deeply ingrained cultural practice among the Tharu, with no stigma attached. Most of the mothers had worked as Kamlaris when they were young, and many of them had been mistreated by their employers. Yet, their families lived in dire poverty, so they understood the economic necessity. Some of the mothers, however, admitted to Som that they were distraught when their daughters left home. One woman recalled the day she dropped her daughter off at the employer's house.

"I left my daughter in the house and went outside. I could hear her sobbing. Outside the house, I was full of tears. Weeping, I tiptoed from the house fearing that my daughter would run out to come home with me." Another mother tearfully told Som that she did not eat for five days after her six-year-old daughter left home to become a Kamlari.

Some of the fathers, however, were quite proud that their daughters were helping to support the family, and even boasted that several of their girls had been contracted away. Typically, the contracts lasted for one year, but many were renewed year after year until the girls reached the age of 16 or 17.

Som encouraged the villagers to bring their daughters home for the festival, assuring them that the foundation would pay for the girls' education if they allowed them to stay home. But he soon realized this was not enough—many families depended on their daughters' wages for their very survival. So he made them a promise: if they kept their daughters at home when they returned for Maghe, we would not only pay for their education, but would compensate the families for the forfeited wages.

When Som returned to Kathmandu, we talked about how we would make up for the girls' wages. One alternative we discussed was to pay the families the amount their daughters would have earned had they fulfilled the labor contract, but nothing was settled before he left again for Dang less than two months later.

The Maghe festival was in full swing when Som arrived, and many young girls had already been sold into bondage. "The streets were filled with motorcycle guys from all over the country, wearing black sunglasses, making deals with the fathers," Som recalls. "The middlemen knew exactly which families had young girls and which doors to knock on." Slick and persuasive, dressed in western clothing, the men persuaded the fathers to sign the contracts. They worked openly and without shame—bargaining, promising and whisking the children away when the deals were concluded. There was no sign of embarrassment about the transactions. Some of the men even bragged openly about being able to buy labor so cheaply.

The girls themselves, frightened and unsure where they would be taken, seemed to realize that their childhoods were at an end. Many begged their parents not to send them away.

Thirty-six of the families Som had spoken with in November brought their daughters home for Maghe. Now it was time to make good on our promises to the families. Instead of immediately offering cash to the fathers to make up for their daughters' wages, Som decided to mosey around the villages and talk to the women. They took him aside and begged him not to give money to their husbands. Alcoholism was rife among the men in the community and the mothers feared that most of the money would be wasted on *rakshi*, the local "white lightning."

He also learned that piglets were highly valued by the Tharus. After some discussion, the women and Som came up with a solution: the foundation would offer each family a piglet in exchange for keeping their daughter at home. They could raise the animal on kitchen scraps and sell it at the end of the year for about as much as their daughters would have earned, or they could breed the piglet and make even more.

One piglet for one girl! It just might work.

The Nepal Youth Foundation enrolled the 36 girls whose fathers had accepted our offer in the local government school. Each girl received a uniform, school supplies and a book bag. Their copybooks were imprinted with the slogan. *Girls deserve an education—not slavery!* In addition to a squealing baby pig, each family received a kerosene lamp and three liters of kerosene a month. The lamp would enable the girls to study at night, as most homes did not have electricity.

The girls who enrolled in the program were also presented with a traditional Tharu dress, one of the most colorful local costumes in Nepal. When middlemen visited the villages for Maghe, they often brought along a few girls who had previously been bonded, dressed in pretty city clothes, to entice the local girls to join them. We hoped that the Tharu costume would provide an antidote to this temptation. On one occasion, their plan backfired. Three little Kamlaris who had been allowed to go home for the festival, decked out in fancy city clothes to tempt their friends to become Kamlari, heard the message against bonding and refused to go back to work.

The following year, I accompanied Som to Dang for the Maghe festival. The visit provoked a roller-coaster of emotions: sadness and anger, but also hope. I was amazed to see how young the girls were, many seven, eight or nine years old. A few of them were only six. Some girls who had returned home for the holiday had rough, red, calloused hands from hard physical labor. The youngest girls cowered behind their mothers, frightened that they, too, were about to be sold.

My most vivid memory of that visit was a conversation with the uncle of a young Kamlari. She was small and frail, and I had a strong sense that she had suffered abuse at the hands of her employer. As she sobbed by her uncle's side, begging to be allowed to stay at home, he told us that he was sending her back to work.

In Nepal, a man is responsible for the care and upbringing of his deceased brother's children if they have no mother. The little Kamlari weeping by her uncle's side was his niece, and she and her sister had come to live with the uncle's family because they were orphans. Within a short time, he sold both of them to work at a home far away from the village. Not so surprising, perhaps, in the Tharu context, but his reason for doing so enrages me to this day. He had sold his two young nieces because he needed the money to pay the expenses for his son's wedding.

We also saw things that lifted our spirits. Many of the villagers were genuinely enthusiastic about the prospect of keeping their daughters at home. Students in the villages, both boys and girls, were eager to help us in our efforts to combat the kamlari practice. Occasionally, a girl simply refused to be shipped off to work—a bold and extraordinary act of defiance in a culture where girls are raised to be passive and obedient. We were thrilled when 150 girls enrolled in the Indentured Daughters Program—the official name of the "piglet-for-a-girl" scheme. This time, parents were offered the choice of a piglet or a baby goat. Some families chose a goat because they were less costly to raise, as they could graze on nearby brush.

We conducted a rather unscientific study to determine how many girls had been bonded away in the five districts where the custom was prevalent and estimated that there were somewhere between 18,000 and 20,000 Kamlaris. With a problem of such magnitude, it was clear that if we wanted to rescue more girls and end the bonding custom, we needed to convince the community that the practice was harmful to their daughters, as well as immoral and illegal. Som and I were busy with foundation work in Kathmandu, and we needed the help of a smart, committed social worker who was willing to live in Western Nepal, get to know the Tharu community and gain their trust.

Man Bahadur Chhetri proved to be the right person for the job. He had a background as a dedicated social worker and a zealous advocate for the rights of girls in Western Nepal, and was familiar with the Tharu community and its culture. Man Bahadur was the consummate iron hand in the velvet glove. His demeanor was mellow and easygoing, but when it came to defending the rights of children, he had a steely, single-minded determination. Som and I agreed that he was the fearless leader we needed to promote the anti-bonding cause. He moved to Dang and lived among the Tharu, adopting a simple lifestyle. As we had hoped, he soon gained the respect and trust of the community, the parents of the Kamlaris and the girls themselves.

He was tireless in promoting the anti-bonding campaign. With his help, we engaged local "motivators" - young schoolteachers and others who opposed the bonding practice. We trained them to call on parents of Kamlaris to convince them to bring their daughters home, as well as on families with young girls in danger of being bonded. He arranged for the liberated girls and local motivators to speak to crowds of villagers at community meetings, driving home the message that girls had a right to go to school and that the practice of kamlari was harmful to their daughters. Young girls whose parents were pressuring them to go off to work, or who knew someone in that position, were urged to contact a motivator or the local office of our foundation.

The former Kamlaris became our eyes and ears on the ground in the villages. They joined together to form anti-bonding clubs in the schools. Hundreds of girls throughout the Dang District distributed leaflets and posted notices on tree trunks, buildings and walls, warning of the dangers to girls who were contracted away. Those who were literate spread the message by word of mouth.

During Maghe, club members and other locals stationed themselves along roadways to intercept vehicles that might be carrying away newly-bonded girls. They boarded buses about to leave the area and interrogated passengers who were accompanied by young girls. One group of former Kamlaris learned that several girls who had just been sold were on a bus about to leave for Kathmandu. They banged furiously on the side of the bus, forcing the driver to open the door. Inside, they found six frightened little girls, including a 10-year-old whose mother was weeping at the door. The father had sold the child against the mother's wishes. They shepherded the children off the bus and enrolled them in the Indentured Daughters Program.

As the Nepal Youth Foundation continued to promote the anti-bonding campaign, opposition to the practice mounted within the community. We tried hard to convince the Nepali government to specifically outlaw the kamlari practice. It was already illegal under general laws of Nepal, such as those outlawing child labor, as well as international agreements the country had signed, but there was no statute addressing the issue directly. When we began our campaign, the foundation sought to enlist the help of local and international non-governmental organizations working for children's rights to eradicate the custom. But they took the position that the practice was "only" domestic labor, not slavery. Even though we provided them with evidence of the extent of the practice, the slave-like conditions under which the girls worked and the abuse they suffered, it was an uphill battle. Ultimately, some of these organizations joined the anti-bonding campaign.

Our foundation also pursued legal remedies to fight against the kamlari practice, initiating almost 200 lawsuits and mediations against employers who refused to free Kamlaris. These cases were publicized in local newspapers. We purchased time on a local radio station for a program about the plight of the bonded girls, and it reached many families. During the weekly broadcasts, the liberated girls talked about their suffering, recited poems and sang songs about their ordeal. This was written by a freed Kamlari in the 4th grade.

Father, I beg you
Let me go to school
Father, and my mother
I join my ten fingers
Don't send us to work
For the landlords

Though we are daughters
We are your children
No high caste or low caste
No rich and poor
We are all equal
Let us walk in a good path
Make your children's future bright

Hoping to reach large audiences, we sponsored street plays to dramatize the suffering of the Kamlaris. Because television was not widespread in the area and there was not much other entertainment, we hoped that a real-life drama would evoke curiosity and draw large crowds as the only game in town.

Our foundation recruited 35 of the liberated girls and sent them to the Gurukul drama school in Kathmandu. They worked with a drama coach, sharing stories about the pain and loneliness they had felt in leaving their families at a young age and the suffering they had endured while working as servants far from home. Based on their own life experiences, they composed plays that dramatically depicted what happens when a girl is sent away. These performances recounted shocking conditions of dire poverty, alcoholic fathers, exploitative landlords and female subjugation in a patriarchal society.

In a strange twist of fate, it was the Gurukul brochure that Urmila saw when she was working for "Cruel Ma'am." The photograph of the former Kamlaris performing in a street play to protest the bonding practice inspired her to seek her own freedom.

By the time the girls returned home to their villages, they had become confident, skillful performers. With practice and experience, they often improvised on the spot rather than following a script. They were passionate about their role in helping to bring an end to the bonding practice, and determined to make parents aware of the suffering they were inflicting on their daughters. The presentations varied, but the message was clear: "Do not send your daughters away!"

As the street play begins:

A greedy, exploitative landlord threatens to evict a father from the land he is farming unless he repays his soaring debt.

A stranger with dark sunglasses and slick city clothing shows up in the village during the Maghe festival. Suspecting trouble, the frightened young girls begin to whisper among themselves. They've all heard stories about the middlemen who entice the fathers to sell their daughters to work as servants in faraway places. Is it their turn to be sold as Kamlaris?

The alcoholic father takes cash from the middleman. The daughter begs her father not to sell her. The exhausted, malnourished mother stands by sobbing, helplessly, unable to intervene to prevent her daughter from suffering a fate similar to her own.

The middleman delivers the girl to a wealthy, well-dressed woman who lives in a fancy villa in a large, crowded city. Though loving and devoted to her own two children, the cruel mistress dresses the Kamlari in rags and constantly abuses her. She shouts, "You're just a servant. Don't be so selfish wasting time by looking at yourself in the mirror." Grabbing the girl by the hair, the mistress slaps her across the face. "Get back to work, you worthless dog."

The two young children shout at the girl. "You didn't iron my school uniform! My food is cold! You're just a stupid Kamlari." Pushing the girl to the ground, the children kick her viciously.

The performers often shed real tears, as they recall their own suffering. Sometimes the spectacle becomes so intense that the audience forgets that it is a drama. They are outraged as they witness the brutal punishment inflicted on the Kamlaris. Mothers in the audience weep openly, reliving the trauma of bonding their daughters or their own suffering as Kamlaris. Occasionally, someone in the crowd leaps onto the stage to grab the master, threatening to beat him up.

As the drama reaches an emotional climax, a new character—the narrator—jumps into the ring. The action freezes. The narrator poses questions to the audience:

Who is responsible for the girl's suffering? Who is to blame?

Who should be punished? The greedy landlord? The sleazy middleman? The alcoholic father? The weak mother? The cruel mistress?

How should the play end? What is the solution to stopping this cruel treatment of young girls?

These provocative questions spark heated a discussion as the crowd wrestles with issues of right and wrong. Having witnessed in the play how their daughters are abused physically and verbally, the parents in the audience understand, many for the first time, that it is wrong to sell their daughters. They agree that the only way to end their daughters' suffering is to eradicate the shameful practice of kamlari.

The audience also begins to understand why employers are so cruel to the Kamlaris. They are not accountable to anyone for their behavior and they believe that they "own" the girls they "bought," like objects.

As the street plays drew large audiences throughout the Dang District and the anti-bonding campaign expanded, opposition to the practice began to take root in the local culture. Confronted with the dramatic emotional content of the plays and other evidence of the suffering endured by the Kamlaris, some parents grew ashamed to sell their daughters. Som and I were cautiously optimistic that attitudes about the practice were beginning to change.

Our feeling of optimism that the community was behind our efforts was reinforced by a surprising occurrence—a threat from the Maoist party to shut down the Indentured Daughters Program. In 1996, the Communist Party of Nepal (Maoist) began a civil war to establish a People's Republic. They ultimately controlled most of the countryside, including the areas in West Nepal where the Nepal Youth Foundation was working to end the practice of kamlari. The Maoists were philosophically opposed to foreign aid, especially from the United States, which had classified them as a terrorist organization.

In 2004, one of the local Maoist commanders in Dang summoned Man Bahadur and ordered him to stop his activities and leave the area immediately because, he claimed, the Indentured Daughters Program was supported by the United States government. He had noticed a small, white-haired foreign woman visiting the area from time to time (that's me), and heard that she was an American who had come to Dang to monitor the program. Man Bahadur carefully explained that our program was not funded by the American government, but by the Nepal Youth Foundation, a private organization. He told the commander that the money came from donations from individuals and organizations vehemently opposed to the kamlari practice. The commander was unmoved.

Following this conversation, Man Bahadur called together members of the community—mothers, fathers, freed Kamlaris and others—and told them that the local commander had ordered him to close the Indentured Daughters Program program and leave the area immediately. They were outraged. Who would rescue their daughters, pay for their education and provide them with an animal to make up for the lost wages? They confronted the commander and told him that if he did not change his mind, they would refuse food and shelter to the many Maoists who used the Deukhuri Valley in Dang as a corridor between their headquarters in the adjoining Rolpa District and India.

In response, the commander asked Man Bahadur to travel with him to the Rolpa District to meet his superior who would make the final decision. The two of them walked for a day and a half until they reached a Maoist encampment in Rolpa. Man Bahadur repeated to the commander's boss that the funds to support the Indentured Daughters Program did not come from the American government, but from private individuals, including many women and school children who were sympathetic to the plight of the bonded girls. The white haired lady whose organization was raising the money for the liberation campaign was not an official of the American government.

After a long discussion, the official told Man Bahadur that he was free to continue the program. In fact, he said that our foundation was doing exactly what the Maoists would do if they had the money, and that the white-haired lady was welcome to return to Dang without fear that the Maoists would harm her. After that conversation, we continued to run the Indentured Daughters Program in West Nepal without any further interference from the Maoists. This was a remarkable accomplishment, since few foreign non-governmental organizations were allowed to operate in areas under Maoist control.

The kamlari issue began to attract attention outside Nepal. National Public Radio's NOW program sent a crew to Nepal to film an excellent documentary about the kamlari tradition and the foundation's role in its eradication. ABC News covered the issue, and the *San Francisco Chronicle* published a feature story on the plight of the indentured girls.

In May 2002, I was invited to appear on The Oprah Winfrey Show. I flew to Chicago, and after an overnight stay at a hotel, was whisked by limo to Oprah's studio. There was a brief session with a makeup artist and hairstylist before I was ushered into the studio, where a small audience was waiting. Oprah entered, greeted everyone, and began to chat with the audience before the show began. She is as funny, warm and approachable in person as she is on television. With Oprah, what you see is what you get. Before the cameras started rolling, during commercial breaks and after the broadcast was over, she engaged in informal chitchat with the audience. She has a genius for creating a one-on-one, intimate connection with others and these exchanges were great fun.

Oprah was primarily interested in talking about the Indentured Daughters Program. The broadcast aired shortly before Mother's Day, and she urged her viewers to save a young Nepali girl from slavery by buying a piglet. Many did so as a Mother's Day gift—a unique present for their moms and the best bargain in the world! For only $100, she told her viewers, they could liberate a girl, send her to school and save her childhood. The widespread publicity following the Oprah Show helped raise awareness and funds from viewers all around the world.

By 2009, nine years after the foundation started the Indentured Daughters Program, we had rescued 3,500 girls from servitude. The $100 cost that Oprah mentioned, in addition to paying for the rescue of a Kamlari and a year of schooling, also helped to support the anti-bonding campaign. A key aspect of our efforts was empowerment of the liberated girls. Once they understood their rights, they were no longer timid, compliant little girls acquiescing to their own bondage and became assertive young women who would never be forced into slavery again.

At the Maghe festival that year, the crusade against the kamlari practice reached a milestone. Local officials announced that henceforth, the Dang District would be a "kamlari free zone." From now on law enforcement would cooperate to prevent the bonding of children. Over 2,300 liberated girls marched through the town, shouting exuberantly to celebrate their freedom and the imminent eradication of the kamlari practice in the Dang District. Houses, stores, schools and tree trunks throughout the village were plastered with hand-lettered signs condemning the selling of girls. Marchers waved signs declaring:

Send daughters to school.
This village is free of bonded laborers — the pride of our community.
Girls in this village are not for sale.

I joined the girls, marching and chanting in Nepali. "End the kamlari system" we shouted, shaking our fists in the air. It was thrilling to witness the remarkable transformation these young women had made from slave girls to school girls to social activists.

I must admit, however, that several times during the march I thought to myself, *How did a little girl from the Bronx end up here?*

CHAPTER THREE

OLGA'S PROMISE

I was born with wanderlust in my soul. When I was a teenager growing up in the Bronx, I hated living in New York City—the crowded streets, the noise, the boredom of being stuck in an immigrant community when the whole world was waiting to be discovered. I constantly dreamed of escaping.

My passion for travel was ignited by a high school classmate from Trinidad who entertained me for hours with colorful stories about her life on the tropical Caribbean island. I rattled on so often about my dream of visiting the island that my family nicknamed me "Trinidad." I had to go there!

Sometimes I took the subway to Grand Central Station, that great, cavernous, reverberating space, just to watch the constant stream of people rushing around, bidding their good-byes, bound for who-knows-where. I was mesmerized by the big destination board that clicked incessantly with announcements of departures to impossibly distant and exotic places while the loudspeaker broadcasted destinations in an almost incomprehensible monotone. I imagined myself boarding a train to Minneapolis, Buffalo, St. Louis—anywhere far from New York. I sighed with longing—and took the subway home.

It was not until much later that I was finally able to satisfy my longing to see the world. I spent many vacations exploring Europe and Central America, returning often to my favorite destination, the Greek Islands. In 1984, ready for a change of perspective and a new adventure, I decided to take a six-week trip to India. On a whim, I bought a ticket for a side trip to Nepal, even though I knew nothing about the country except that it was possible to trek in the beautiful Himalayas, and I loved to hike.

I realized it would be an enormous physical challenge to get in shape for the trek. Approaching the age of 60, I was not very athletic and had been largely sedentary for a long time, and balance was a bit dicey. Yet I was blessed with excellent health and good endurance, so I thought that somehow I could make it over the mountains if I had enough time to get in shape.

With a full-time, demanding job, I knew that the only way I would be able to get fit would be to incorporate exercise into my daily routine. Three days a week, I walked nine miles across the Golden Gate Bridge from my home in Sausalito to my job in San Francisco, carrying my formal work clothes and shoes in a little backpack. It took three hours door to door, but I arrived promptly at nine every morning, in time for work. Still, the thought of walking many miles a day over remote mountain trails in a country I knew little about scared me.

I left for India in September 1984, and traveled alone from Delhi around the country by air, train and bus. India and its people proved to be an astonishing revelation. I had some extraordinary experiences, including a trek by camel in the Thar Desert on the Pakistan border, and a friendship with a man I later discovered was one of the most violent criminals in the country. It was the most intense, difficult, frustrating, fascinating place I had ever been—utterly compelling, utterly exhausting.

After several weeks, I boarded a plane for the one-hour flight to Kathmandu. I had no inkling that I was about to embark on an adventure that would change the course of my life.

Rudyard Kipling knew what he was talking about when he said in a poem, "The wildest dreams of Kew are the facts of Kathmandu." This is true, even today.

My first view of Kathmandu was magical. The city is studded with temples, large and small. Buddhists and Hindus worship at the same shrines. Early in the morning, the locals make offerings, ringing temple bells over the honking of horns and lighting incense amid diesel exhaust. Exquisite centuries-old woodcarvings adorn crumbling buildings. In alleys tucked between tea houses, children and adults disabled by polio or leprosy beg for rupees. The traffic is unbelievably chaotic.

A casual stroll through the streets might bring you face to face with a cow or two stopping traffic in the middle of a crowded street, a man herding goats to slaughter, buck-naked babies being bathed from plastic pails, or *sadhus* (holy men) with their long, dreadlocked hair, barely clothed, covered with white ash, their tin begging bowls at the ready.

Despite the overwhelming poverty, what impressed me most was the air of buoyancy and friendliness of the people I saw on the street. They seemed to have an innate joy, which took me by surprise. It was almost love at first sight—not with a man, but with a country.

The trek began in the city of Pokhara, a short flight from Kathmandu. With a crew of porters, cooks and guides, my two fellow trekkers and I hiked along steep trails over legendary mountains to Siklis, at 12,000 feet. As we passed through beautiful villages, some of which had not changed in centuries, we encountered the most cheerful people eking out a primitive existence among stunning surroundings. I was charmed by their freshness, curiosity and innocence.

Trekking in Nepal is not for the self-conscious, or at least it wasn't 30 years ago. In rural Nepal, it was not considered rude to stare at a stranger. The locals we met on the trail sometimes stopped in their tracks, transfixed, until we were out of sight. I assumed it was my age and white hair that so startled them. Once, I heard someone running behind me; an elderly, toothless man, cap askew, wearing a torn shirt, stepped right in front of me on the trail, forcing me to stop suddenly. He brought his face close to mine, stared intensely for a moment, and then ran down the trail, slapping his thigh, bent over with laughter.

The children along the trail captivated me. They were dressed in tattered, dirty clothes, thin, much smaller than western children their age, yet they were the most joyful kids I had ever seen. They came in bunches, five, six, seven at a time, many carrying smaller children on their backs. Some were shy. Others placed their hands together and called out the traditional greeting, *"Namaste,"* over and over. Sometimes, whole troops of kids followed us, vying to hold our hands, laughing at anything we said or did. When I tried out my 10 words of Nepali, they laughed so hard that I thought they would fall off the trail. We could not understand each other, but it didn't matter.

When we camped near a village, I would unzip the flap of my tent at dawn to find three or four little faces peering through the opening, hoping to catch a glimpse of the strange creature inside. All our possessions were the subject of intense curiosity: toothpaste, toothbrushes, sleeping bags and every piece of clothing. The biggest hit was the small mirror I carried in my pack. Mirrors were not a common item in the villages of Nepal and most of the children had never seen their own faces. They found their reflections hilarious.

As we walked along, they babbled on in Nepali, unfazed by the fact that we had no idea what they were saying. Sometimes, the guides translated their words. Throughout those 10 days we spent slogging along the trail, every child said the same thing when I asked them about their lives: what they wanted most in the world was to go to school. In 1984, most children in Nepal did not attend school.

One evening, while camping near a hut on top of a small mountain, I was invited inside for a visit. Three young children were sitting on the dirt floor doing their homework by candlelight, their notebooks resting on a crude wooden plank that served as a desk. Their father and I were able to communicate through a few halting words in Nepali. His children were the lucky ones, he told me. Even though they walked two hours up and down the mountain to reach school every day, they were getting an education.

Lying in my sleeping bag that night in the darkness of the tent, I suddenly knew—out of the blue, in a lightning moment—what I wanted to do with the rest of my life. Right then, I made a promise to myself that I would find a way to educate Nepali children.

The idea took root immediately and remained constantly in my thoughts. Even after my return to California, I knew in my heart that I wanted to pursue my mountaintop vision and realized I could not continue to work indefinitely. A few years down the road I would have to retire, and I was certain that when the time came, I did not want to spend my days playing bridge, shopping and lunching with friends. I had always known that I would work with children when I retired, but I was not clear how. Perhaps I would be an advocate for youngsters in juvenile court or a tutor at a community center center in a disadvantaged neighborhood. Now, I realized that what I really wanted to do was to make a positive difference in the lives of children halfway across the world. I had no idea how I could do this in a country and culture so different from my own, but the only way I could find out was to go back to Nepal to explore the possibilities.

When I returned to Kathmandu the following year, a friend introduced me to Allan Aistrope, a volunteer English teacher at Paropakar Orphanage, Nepal's first orphanage. Allan had been working in advertising for an oil company in San Francisco when he decided to take a year off to teach in Nepal. He fell in love with Nepalese children and stayed on helping the boys at the orphanage by teaching English and finding college scholarships for those who finished high school. He was a father figure to them all, and they loved and respected him.

I will never forget my first visit to Paropakar. To get there, we walked through the bazaar, where everything under the sun was sold outdoors. Vibrant, nearly fluorescent colored spices were displayed alongside goat meat advertised by a goat's head out front dyed bright orange. There were piles of scrawny chickens with their legs raised high in the air, copper and brass pots, mountains of strange-looking fruits and vegetables stacked on the steps of ancient temples, below stone lions frozen in mid-snarl. Amid the chaos, customers haggled over the price of cauliflower or potatoes.

Threading through the crowd were flute sellers tootling away. Serene Buddhist monks with shaved heads, wearing scarlet robes, seemed unfazed by the commotion. Porters carried everything imaginable, from closets to sweaters, bent double under their heavy loads. We passed the street of tooth pullers and the ancient toothache tree where locals believed that your toothache would disappear if you nailed a coin into the bark. All this by candlelight; as often still happens in Kathmandu, the street and shop lights were out due to the scarcity of electricity.

The orphanage was housed in a dilapidated old building located in one of the most crowded, noisy, polluted areas of the city, on the banks of a filthy river. There were only a couple of taps with cold water for washing, and all the boys slept in one room. They played in a narrow alley confined by a high wall at the back of the building and seldom left the premises except to go to school across the street.

As I entered the candle-lit classroom, 50 boys, ages six through sixteen, sat quietly on the floor, their legs crossed, awaiting me. It was an awkward moment. I smiled and said hello. The boys greeted me in unison. Silence. Then one of the boys pulled out a flute, another ran for a cylindrical drum called a *madel*, and they began singing, dancing and clapping. All were smiling joyously, lost in the moment. I was smitten.

I learned a lot about the boys that night. They felt fortunate to have food, shelter and the opportunity to attend school, and they realized that they were far better off than thousands of children who had nowhere to live but the streets. Yet, after high school, which ends at 10th grade in Nepal, they would have to leave the orphanage, totally unprepared for life outside its walls. In Nepalese society, family connections mean everything, but these boys had no relatives to help them. It was unlikely they would go on to higher education and their prospects for employment were dim.

When I asked Allan what would happen to the boys once they left the orphanage, he explained that if they passed the college entrance exam and were lucky enough to find a sponsor, they could go to college. I asked how many boys would be taking the exam that year.

"Four," Allan replied.

"And how much does it cost to support a student in college?" I asked.

"$300 a year."

"I'll take four," I said.

With those three words and an investment of $1,200, Allan and I launched a scholarship program that would eventually educate many thousands of Nepali children.

When I returned to my job in California, I felt that I had taken only the tiniest step toward my goal. I was itching to visit Nepal again to find out if I could help more children.

In 1987, I returned with two objectives: to spend as much time as I could with the boys at Paropakar and to go on a trek in the Helambu area of the Himalayas with several friends. Prior to the trek, Allan and I spent every afternoon with the boys when they returned from school. He taught English classes for several hours, while I spent my time fooling around, teasing them and leading conga lines through Allan's classroom.

On my first visit, the Paropakar children had impressed me as unselfish, fun-loving and good-natured. This was only reinforced after a two-year absence. With virtually no adult supervision, they provided one another with a tremendous amount of support, the older boys acting as wise and loving big brothers to the younger ones.

Their selflessness was apparent when we distributed clothes from the United States which are highly valued in Nepal. Although ready-made garments are available in the local shops, they are expensive and pretty shoddy.

Clothes-distribution night at Paropakar was a lively and uplifting occasion. We would hold up a pair of pants, a shirt or a jacket, look around the room, and call up a suitably sized kid for the garment. None of them—not a one—ever asked for anything. Instead, as we were getting to the bottom of the bag, someone would push a boy forward, calling out, "Deepak needs a pair of pants," or "Ishwor got only a shirt." Actually, it hardly mattered who got what, because the boys shared everything, including their clothing, without regard to size or fit.

After a few weeks hanging out with the boys at Paropakar, it was time for the trek. I had heard about a *sirdar* (trek leader) named Thundup Sherpa Lama, who had grown up in Namche Bazaar, the largest town on the way to Mt. Everest. In his 40s, Thundup was mellow, cheerful and capable, with many years of experience leading hikers through the Himalayas. He was a deeply religious Buddhist, chanting prayers from his tent at dawn every morning. As the sirdar, he was responsible for the wellbeing of the hikers. He arranged for all the equipment (tents, sleeping bags, cooking gear), hired the staff (cooks, guides, porters) and planned the daily hike. The porters carried the equipment, as well as the hikers' gear and clothing, on their backs in a basket called a *doko*. Slightly oval in shape, it tapered from a wide opening at the top to a narrow bottom, and was secured by a tumpline around the porter's forehead.

We traveled by jeep with Thundup to the town of Sundarijal, where we met our crew and began our walk. On the third day of the trek, as we walked along a fairly level trail at moderate altitude, Thundup warned us to be careful because we were approaching an area covered in red mud that was as slick as ice. Chatting with one of my friends who was walking behind me, I slipped and fell. I tried to get up, but could not put weight on my left leg without excruciating pain. It was clear that something was seriously wrong. My friends suggested that we all return to Kathmandu, but I would have none of it. They had traveled thousands of miles to get there and I was determined that they would finish the trek. Somehow, I would find a way to get back to Kathmandu.

While we were debating, Thundup, without a word, pulled a long, strong rope out of his pocket, relieved us of our hiking sticks (which were really just small branches we had picked up along the way), and fashioned a crude ladder that he affixed with the rope to the back of a *doko*. He filled the basket with sleeping bags and topped it off with a comfortable air mattress. Problem solved: everyone would finish the trek, while I rode in style in the basket, carried by a porter.

For seven days, four porters took turns carrying me over the rugged mountain trails. I was terrified the first day as we crossed several tottering bridges—or what passed for bridges in rural Nepal. Some were rickety structures barely three feet wide, the surface a few flimsy wooden boards with gaps between them, the sides a thin piece of rope or a wire. As we crossed, the bridge would wobble and creak. Below raced the wild, roaring rivers of the Himalayas. In some spots the trail was so narrow that the porters were just a foot or two away from the edge of the cliff. Several times, I found myself hanging over a precipice as the porter turned a corner.

I tossed and turned in my sleeping bag that first night, unable to sleep. The stress of the day's journey had taken a toll. *What if the porter loses his footing? What if the ladder made of our hiking sticks isn't tied securely to the basket? What if the load of two people together on the fragile bridges is too much?* I knew that a single misstep by the porter could send us tumbling headlong over a steep cliff or into a thundering river. After a few hours of contemplating these disasters, I realized that I had only two options. I could have a nervous breakdown, or I could trust the porters and enjoy the experience. I chose the latter. When the porter arrived with the basket in the morning, I greeted him with a smile, looking forward to the day's journey.

For seven days I was carried over the mountains like a princess, wearing dark glasses, with a black umbrella shading me and my left leg wrapped in a dark green garbage bag. What I remember most vividly is not the heart-stopping scenery or the medicine man/porter who chanted mysterious incantations over my ankle each night as he rubbed cigarette ashes into it to "cure" me, but the cheerfulness, tender care and cooperative spirit of the porters. My life was quite literally in their hands—or rather their feet. I weighed 125 pounds, and together with the basket, ladder and sleeping bags, the porters were carrying at least 140 pounds, as much as some of them weighed. Yet their prime concern was my comfort and safety, as they cautiously placed one foot in front of another along the trail. My job was to sit as still as I could so as not to disturb the delicate balance.

Thundup walked alongside, chatting briefly with locals we met on the trail. After a while, I realized that some of the conversations sounded alike. When I asked him what they were saying, he replied, "They want to know what is the matter with you. 'Is the old lady sick?' they are asking?"

"And what are you telling them?"

"I tell them, no. She's just rich and lazy!" My first exposure to Sherpa humor.

The porters sang and joked as they walked along. When one got tired, he stopped, placed me on a ledge and helped his fellow porter take up the burden. I never heard a cross word among them, much less an argument about how long each one had carried me. There was one older porter who groaned occasionally under the load. How ashamed I was when this happened, wishing I had the power of levitation. At night, the porters and other members of the crew cooked *dal bhat/ tarkari*, the Nepali staple dish of rice, lentils and vegetables. After the meal, they sang and danced around their campfire. I was amazed and moved by their joyfulness and willingness to share the burden without complaint, in the face of what others would consider to be intolerable circumstances. The seven days I spent riding in that basket deepened my respect and affection for the people of Nepal.

For most of that time I was alone with my thoughts, as my friends walked ahead or behind us. Perhaps to keep my mind off my precarious situation, I began to reflect on the journey that had brought me here, riding high in a basket filled with sleeping bags, carried through the Himalayas on the backs of porters, my life dependent on their strength and stability.

Tharu village in Southwestern Nepal

Middlemen arrive in the villages on motorbikes to buy young girls to work as kitchen slaves

Photo by Carlos Avila Gonzalez, SF Chronicle, Pulitzer Center for Crisis Reporting

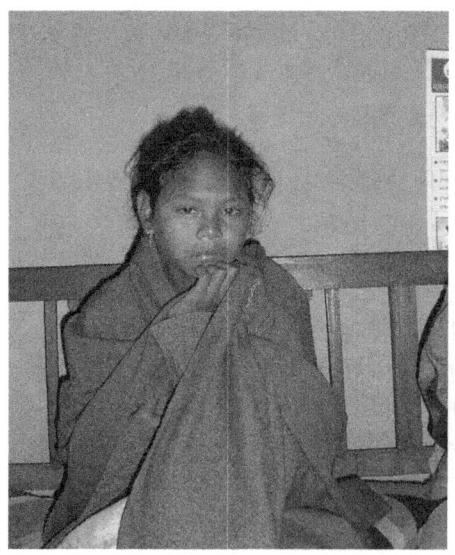

Ten year old girl rescued from a bus, as she was being sent away to work as a Kamlari

Young girls liberated from bondage

Audience reaction

Freed girls performing in a street play to protest the kamlari practice

Crowd watching a play

Tharu girl reading
anti-bonding message
to mothers

Freed Kamlari holding her new goat

School girls with their goats

Prospective Kamlaris listening
to anti-bonding message

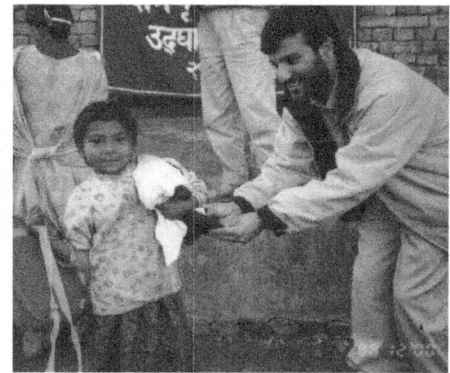

Som distributes school supplies
to a little ex-Kamlari

Liberated girls eager to learn
after years of bondage

Ex-kamlaris attend
a literacy class

Released from bondage and
on their way to school

It's always a joy to spend time
with the freed Kamlaris

My first anti-bonding march

Photo by Carlos Avila Gonzales,
SF Chronicle, Pulitzer
Center for Crisis Reporting

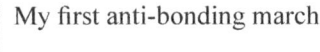

The chaotic streets of Kathmandu
Photo by Hans Knikman

Trekking in the beautiful Himalayas, 1984

Adorable Nepali children along the trail. They all told us they wanted to go to school

A darling little girl on the trail

We crossed many rickety bridges during the trek. This one was fairly stable!

Trekking 1987 – That little white dot is me riding in a *doko*

Allan Aistrope and me

Boys at Paropakar Orphanage

Carried through the mountains

Here I am leading a conga line of Paropakar boys

CHAPTER FOUR

LITTLE GIRL FROM THE BRONX

My journey to the Bronx at the age of six was a long and circuitous odyssey from Transylvania, where I was born. Our family traveled by train to Cherbourg, France, where we boarded the SS Leviathan, the largest passenger ship of its time. We traveled in steerage, crowded onto a lower deck of the ship with hundreds of other immigrants heading for the land of opportunity.

On June 6, 1931, we arrived in New York on a beautiful, sunny day. Sailing into the harbor, I stood on the deck of the launch with my mother and my three siblings. As we approached the shore, my mother Matilda pointed to a man waving from the dock. *"Az apuka,"* she said in Hungarian. "That's your daddy."

Four years earlier, in 1927, my father Joseph had immigrated to the United States from Transylvania, a territory ceded by Hungary to Romania after World War I. A large population of ethnic Hungarians, including our family, lived in the region. I was just two years old when he left for America.

My father was a skilled craftsman. Starting at the age of seven, he learned as an apprentice how to build and upholster exquisite furniture. A year after arriving in New York City with $38 dollars and his violin, he opened a shop as a furniture maker on Third Avenue in Manhattan.

At the first opportunity four years later, he applied for American citizenship and bought passage on the *Leviathan* so that we could join him. As we disembarked in the harbor, he beamed with pride, welcoming his wife and four children to our new home. Not only were we settling into a new country, we had a new name. When my father had arrived at Ellis Island in 1927, the officer who interviewed him, tired of spelling out his long name—Davidovits—assigned him a new one on the spot. So we were now the Davis kids: Bertha (four years old), Olga (six), Shirley (eight), and Alex (ten).

We moved into a comfortable, beautifully furnished home in the Bronx that my father had prepared for us—quite a contrast to our little two-room cottage with a dirt-floored kitchen in Romania. But Bertha and I hardly took notice of the improvement because of an outrageous act of betrayal committed by our mother. During the four years my father was away, we had shared a cozy bed with her. Now she insisted on doubling up with this stranger and exiling us to a bedroom of our own. We complained for days before we got over this double-cross.

My parents were an unusual pair. My father had fallen in love with my mother, a beauty, the minute he set eyes on her. He proposed to her a couple of weeks later, and they were married in 1919, not long after he returned from military duty at the end of World War I. He had served on three fronts in the army of the Austro-Hungarian Empire, suffering gunshot wounds to his leg that pained him for many years.

It was a love affair that lasted more than 59 years, until my father died in 1978. I don't recall a harsh word between them: no arguments, no criticism, no nagging. Somehow, whatever disagreements they might have had were worked out in private. My siblings and I grew up in a peaceful, loving environment. Our parents' example did not keep us from the usual childhood bickering, but those early spats did not harm our relationship. We remained close and supportive of one another throughout our lives.

At the time we settled into our new home, my father was the only one in the family who spoke English. He had taught himself to do so by reading *The New York Times* every day, translating unfamiliar words with an English-Hungarian dictionary by his side, and copying them into a notebook. Through curiosity and single-minded determination, he became an articulate English speaker with an excellent vocabulary. *The New York Times* was a revered object in the Davis household, and no other newspaper was allowed in our home.

At first, we kids wanted to huddle together in the house, talking to one another in Hungarian, but my parents shooed us outside to play with children in the neighborhood. When school started three months later, we all spoke unaccented English fluently—witness to the power of language immersion. The only misstep I remember was a time when my brother Alex was playing stickball with some boys in the street. When they yelled at him to "run home, run home," he ran, terrified, up the stairs of our house and through the front door.

After a few years, our family moved to another apartment in the Bronx, on Prospect Avenue. Our neighborhood was primarily populated by immigrants from southern Europe. Many worked in factories or small shops, and some were craftsmen like my father. Most of the buildings on our street had six or eight apartments, with a stoop out front that became a focal point in our lives. This was where most of our neighbors sat on summer nights to avoid the stifling heat inside the building, where our parents met and gossiped if they had leisure time and where we kids played. The mélange of accents was breathtaking: Italian, Russian, Hungarian, Polish, to name a few. I don't recall a single friend whose parents had been born in the United States.

Halloween was a favorite holiday. We kids gathered on the stoop to begin our forays around the neighborhood. For most of my childhood, my costume was a long black dress of heavy cotton with a high neck and long sleeves that my mother made for me when I played the role of the Ant in our 2nd grade school play, *The Grasshopper and the Ant*. A tall pointed hat made of black crepe paper topped off my witch costume. I usually won the tussle with my siblings to carry our family's sole broom. We filled long cotton stockings with powdered chalk and ventured forth, threatening front doors and cars with immediate desecration if the owners didn't pony up.

We played ball, hopscotch and double-dutch jump rope on the sidewalk. On the few occasions when an airplane flew overhead, we stopped what we were doing to gaze skyward in wonder. I loved to roller skate and would get up early in the morning to get in an hour of gliding along the empty streets before school started. Our favorite Saturday-night treat was a stroll down the street to get ice cream cones, which we ate on the lawn of a neighborhood church.

The four of us attended New York public schools and did well academically. My father and mother were ardent supporters of President Franklin Roosevelt, and conversation often focused on politics and social issues as we sat around the kitchen table for breakfast and dinner. We gathered by the radio in the living room to listen to the President's periodic fireside chats to the American people, my parents sitting on the couch, the kids on the floor. Ever since, I have maintained a keen interest in politics.

My father was a great storyteller. He had excellent timing and punctuated his tales with laughter and little asides. We listened for hours as he recounted stories of his childhood in Hungary and his early days in the United States. One of our favorites was his tale about the time he stole a ditch-digger's jacket.

When he left Romania, my mother, an expert seamstress, made a coat that she thought would be fashionable in the New World. She wanted her man to start out right. It was long, black and somber, made of the finest wool, beautifully stitched, topped off with a luxurious brown fur collar. It didn't take long after he arrived in New York for my father to realize how freakish he looked—passersby stared, a few pointed and sometimes they laughed. He was embarrassed and uncomfortable, but the coat was warm and made by my mother's own loving hands—and New York was freezing in February.

One afternoon, as he was walking along Third Avenue, he saw several workmen digging up the sidewalk. Nearby, their shabby, battered jackets hung on the branches of a tree. He noticed an ancient scratched leather jacket just his size. In a flash, he grabbed it, removed his own coat, hung it on the same tree limb and took it on the lam. No matter how many times he told the story of this daring feat, we still had a good laugh at the thought of the bewildered workman returning to fetch his tattered jacket on his lunch break, and magically finding instead a long, black wool coat with a fluffy fur collar.

During the 1930s, when the United States was in the depths of the Great Depression, our family struggled, as did most of our neighbors. My parents took pride in not relying on government assistance, even when my mother had trouble putting food on the table. Occasionally, she sent us to the grocery store, our arms filled with empty milk bottles, to redeem the deposit so she could buy food for dinner. Our parents seldom spoke to us about their financial difficulties, but we sometimes heard them discussing how they would pay the bills, and we were aware that our mother occasionally had to ask the grocer for credit. The atmosphere in our house was usually cheerful, but we kids knew at the deepest level of our being that our parents struggled daily to provide us with the things we needed to grow up healthy and whole. All four of us were determined to become financially independent as soon as we were able.

Even though they struggled financially, my parents were givers: tolerant, kind and generous with their meager funds. My mother kept a drawer full of solicitation envelopes and would send in a donation whenever she had an extra $5 to spare.

Our apartment building on Prospect Avenue was owned by Mr. Napolitano, who came to collect the rent on the first Saturday of the month. He was a wondrous sight in our neighborhood, where workmen dressed casually, to say the least. Not Mr. Napolitano. He appeared in an impeccably tailored three-piece suit, highly polished shoes, a starched shirt collar, a beautiful homburg resting on his perfectly barbered white hair. All this was topped off with a splendid silver moustache. On the few Saturdays when my parents did not have enough money to pay the rent, we kids were ordered to lean out the window and watch for Mr. Napolitano as he came down the street, tapping his cane. We would sound the alarm when we spotted him, then pop our heads back inside and stay perfectly silent as he rang the bell over and over again to collect his just dues. The poor man would return the following Saturday, by which time my parents had somehow cobbled together the money for another month's rent.

Despite my father's many talents, he was an indifferent businessman and the task of holding the family together financially fell to my mother. She was an accomplished seamstress and made beautiful draperies and slipcovers that were in high demand among my father's wealthy customers. My mother made many of our clothes, sometimes from leftover slipcover material, perfectly tailored, though often the fabric was more suited to slipcovers than children's dresses. My sisters and I used to tease our mother, "What if Mrs. Rich Lady sees us wearing her slipcover?"

To make ends meet, my mother worked incessantly. She cooked and cleaned house for the six of us in the days before there were microwave ovens or affordable fast food. Her old-fashioned treadle sewing machine rumbled on late into the night. The constant cry in our household was, "Go to sleep, Mama!" Frequently, the neighbor in the downstairs apartment knocked on the ceiling with a broom handle to signal his displeasure at the late-night disturbance. We kids put our heads under the covers to deaden the noise so we could sleep.

If there were a Nobel Prize for listening, my parents would have been winners. Every eccentric in the neighborhood came calling at my father's shop to take advantage of his sympathetic ear. On and on they droned, hour after hour, as my father went about his work, making small sympathetic sounds now and then. My mother also entertained an odd cast of characters, who felt welcome in her kitchen. We kids would come home from school to find an unhappy visitor jabbering away, my mother listening with a full heart, offering advice, comfort and material help when needed. She never displayed a hint of irritation or a desire to see the back of the visitor. To our dismay, she often invited these characters to stay for dinner.

Our parents seldom preached to us, but their example of compassion, hard work, harmony and good cheer was not lost on us. Those were the days before it was considered important to cultivate self-esteem in young children. Although my mother and father seldom praised us directly, we were aware that they were proud of us, each for different qualities, as a result of long bouts of eavesdropping. My brother Alex was a talented musician and a good older brother; my sister Shirley was the saint of the family, the surrogate mother. Bertha was the youngest, the prettiest, and the adorable family pet. They always referred to me as the smart one. Never pretty, just smart — and rather naughty.

One day, when I was 13 years old, I confronted my mother in the living room on a Saturday, the Sabbath, the only day she allowed herself relief from her labors. "Mama," I asked, "am I pretty?" I've thought of this conversation many times and the dilemma she faced in answering my question. She could not very well say that I was beautiful because I knew it wasn't true. And of course, she didn't want to tell me that I wasn't pretty, or sound lukewarm on the subject, because she knew that was not what I needed to hear. She looked at me tenderly, stroked my hair and said softly, "You're beautiful, but you don't know it. Do you realize how your eyes shine, what perfectly arched eyebrows you have, how thick and smooth your hair is, how gracefully you move?" and she went on to describe attributes that most young people share. The next time I looked in the mirror, I knew she was right. Ever since, when I meet a self-conscious, insecure teenager, I want to provide the same assurance my wise, compassionate mother offered to me in that conversation more than 75 years ago.

Although we lived in poverty, we were surrounded by possessions that once belonged to millionaires. Drawn to my father's sparkly personality and easy manner, his wealthy customers showered him with spectacular possessions they no longer wanted. I grew up with boxed sets of Shakespeare, leather-bound encyclopedias, trunks full of French lace and silver trinkets embossed with the names of other children. One millionaire customer who had befriended my father when he first established his business offered him a spare Rolls-Royce with needlepoint seat covers made in Belgium and an outside chauffeur's compartment. My father politely refused this lavish but impractical gift. "What would I do with such a car in the Bronx?" he asked.

He did love beautiful things, though. His shop was open for only half a day on Saturday, and he often spent the afternoon strolling down 57th Street visiting galleries, eager to educate himself about art. Occasionally he bartered his furniture for paintings. Some artists who would eventually become world-renowned were eager to make a deal with him. Many years later, when my father was in his 70s, I mentioned that I had just seen an exhibit of Georgia O'Keeffe paintings. "Oh, her," my father huffed. "I don't like her work. She wanted to exchange one of those big flower pictures for a chair in the '30s, and I wouldn't go for it." He was surprised when I expressed consternation. "I saw no reason to do it," he said. "Just not my taste."

Culture and learning were an important part of our family life. My father was a born enthusiast—a musician, an expert chess player, a passionate photographer and later, an obsessed gardener. He had a sophisticated taste in music. When he was a young boy in Hungary, he taught himself to play the violin well enough to accompany silent films at the local movie theater. At my parents' wedding, he was determined to have music, but could not afford to hire musicians. Never one to let a lack of money deter him, he first vowed his eternal devotion to my mother in marriage, and then picked up the violin so guests could dance to the csardas, a traditional Hungarian folk dance. When he immigrated, he brought his violin with him and entertained his fellow passengers in the ship's steerage with Hungarian and classical violin solos.

I can't remember a time when our home was not filled with classical music playing on the radio or phonograph. My siblings and I all played musical instruments. I took up the violin. My father told us that his mother wouldn't allow him to practice in the house when he was teaching himself to play the violin because it was too painful to listen to the screeching sounds he made. He often pointed out that we kids should thank our lucky stars that we were not only provided with music lessons, but allowed—even encouraged—to practice indoors. On Sunday evenings, we often played quartets with visiting musician friends.

My father took cello lessons well into his 80s and practiced religiously for an hour or more a day, convinced, until almost the end of his life, that he was improving his technique and musicianship. For decades, he played the cello in various community orchestras with other amateur musicians. In his later years, he played in a quartet with three other elderly men.

Through a barter arrangement with the president of Columbia Records, my father acquired a large collection of 33-rpm records of classical music in exchange for his beautiful furniture. He had a groupie's passionate devotion to Pablo Casals, the famous cellist, not only for his superb musicianship but also for his principled stand against fascism in Spain. My father owned every recording Casals ever made. For inspiration, he kept a personally autographed photo of the great man at his side as he practiced. It was one of his most precious possessions.

But there was a cloud over our household. My father and mother worried constantly about the fate of their families who remained in Hungary, Romania and France after Hitler came to power in Germany. I remember my tiny mother lugging large boxes filled with clothes, food and medicine to the post office to send to family overseas. When World War II broke out in Europe, my parents lost contact with their families. Since we were Jewish, they had more to worry about than most. My mother had frequent nightmares rooted in anxiety about the survival of our relatives. Her concerns were well founded. Nine family members, including my father's entire immediate family and my mother's mother, brother and several sisters were murdered in the Holocaust. My family owed its survival to my father's enterprise and resourcefulness in embarking for America, dirt poor, but filled with ambition and optimism. For her part, my mother encouraged this reckless venture, even though it meant that she was left behind—nine months pregnant and virtually penniless—with a brood of young children to raise on her own. Bertha, my little sister, was born four days after my father left the country. He had to cross the Romanian border before January 1 or his visa would have expired.

My father was an eternal optimist. He firmly believed that all his wishes would be fulfilled, and so they were. For many years, while our parents struggled financially, he dreamed of buying land in the countryside where he could plant a large vegetable garden. Every Sunday, he scoured the classified ads in the *Times* looking for farms for sale. Then he would hop into his big, old jalopy, often with me beside him, and head to rural New Jersey or upstate New York to take a look.

He finally found a four-acre former cucumber farm at the end of a road in Westchester County, not far from New York City. The asking price was a steep $3,500. Always practical, my mother protested that they had only $1,500 in the bank. "Besides," she told my father, "respectable people don't borrow money."

But his dream of buying the farm was so palpable that my mother finally relented. They borrowed some money, bought the property and remodeled an old shack into a comfortable, beautiful home, room by room, as they were able to afford it. The land was level and fertile. There was a stream bordering one side of the property with tables and chairs under a big tree for reading, relaxing and dreaming, and a large stone terrace outside the kitchen. My father planted a magnificent vegetable garden and my mother won many prizes for the most gorgeous dahlias in the county.

Our parents planned that their children would learn to make a living the same way they did: we would be apprenticed after high school to the most experienced, accomplished people they could find to train us for a successful career. Alex would learn the furniture business at my father's shop and Shirley, the artistic star of the family, would be apprenticed to a fashion designer. For no particular reason that I could discern—except that my father had recently become enamored with photography—I would be trained as a photographer. No plans had yet been made for Bertha, the youngest in the family. There was no mention of the possibility of college for any of us.

My father had recently bought himself a big old wooden camera with a bellows. True to his nature, he threw himself passionately into his new hobby. I spent many long Sunday afternoons in the park at his side taking pictures of pigeons perched on water fountains, as he encouraged me to be aware of angles, light and composition. He developed and printed his own pictures. The only bathroom in our apartment served as a darkroom, with a black cloth draped over the door to block any light from entering and to prevent any of the stinky chemical vapors from escaping. Two chairs in the tub anchored a board on which the developing fluids sloshed in baking pans.

"Daddy, I have to go to the bathroom," was a constant refrain in our household.

"Not now," my father would respond, "the picture is not fixed yet."

Sometime later, my father became friendly with Louise Dahl-Wolfe, a prominent fashion photographer. He made furniture for the elegant photographs she created for the covers of *Harper's Bazaar*. When I was 15, he asked Ms. Dahl-Wolfe if he could bring me to a photo shoot so I could observe a professional photographer at work. If the visit went well, he planned to ask her about an apprenticeship. We were ushered into an enormous, high-ceilinged room buzzing with cameras. Lights beamed down at various angles on the gorgeous model posed on a dais. Ms. Dahl-Wolfe stood at the center of it all, wearing pants (something I'd never seen on a woman before) and shouting commands. If her orders were not obeyed immediately and correctly, she expressed her displeasure in a loud and forceful way. The models and crew seemed intimidated and exhausted, and all of us were somewhat cooked from the lights. I was terrified. When my father and I left an hour later, I had made up my mind—there was no way I was going to be a photographer.

In 1942, a month after the Japanese attacked Pearl Harbor and the U.S. declared war, I graduated from Theodore Roosevelt High

School at the age of 16. Since a career in photography was not an option, my next best choice was to become a secretary. I enrolled at a school in Manhattan where I learned touch-typing, shorthand and other practical office skills. Then, at the age of 17, I did the unthinkable—something no teenager in our circle had ever dared to do. I left home.

CHAPTER FIVE

FINDING MY WAY

In those days few respectable girls left the shelter of their families, except to get married. Despite my parents' vehement objections, scared but determined, and with tears in my eyes, I boarded a train at Grand Central Station, leaving my sobbing mother standing on the platform. With only a small suitcase and a yearning for adventure, I traveled 3,000 miles across the country by train to Los Angeles, the most exotic place I could think of, and the furthest from the Bronx. There was no possibility of flying then. The commercial airline industry was in its infancy; it was wartime and flights were very expensive and few and far between. I saved up money for the trip by squirrelling away every penny I could from a secretarial job. Armed with my newly acquired skills, I found an office job to support myself in Los Angeles.

My career in sunny California ended abruptly after a few months due to a ruptured appendix. When I was discharged from the hospital after two weeks, my mother insisted that she would travel to the West Coast to bring me home. I refused. "I will come home," I promised, "but only if you let me make the trip on my own." I hopped on a Greyhound bus to New York, stopping along the way in New Orleans and other cities.

Not long after my return, the urge to wander hit me again. This time, I took off for Indianapolis. For the next three years, I traveled by bus or train across the United States. I'd land in a town, find a place to stay and support myself with a typing and stenography job. When I got bored, I moved on. My memories of those years are rather vague, but I remember living in a roach-infested apartment in Indianapolis, walking along the street in Kansas City with tears streaming down my face upon learning of President Roosevelt's sudden death, and skipping lunch for weeks to save up for a half-hour flight in a tiny airplane at a small, dusty airport just outside Kansas City—my first airplane flight.

At one job, I worked for a boss who wrote his letters painstakingly by hand, in pencil. He would rush over, throw the letter on my desk, and shout, "English it! English it!" Over the years, I "Englished" many letters, thanks to the good education provided by the New York City public school system.

In 1945, not long before World War II ended, I took a job at the Fitzsimmons Army Hospital in Denver. I was thrilled to be in the Wild West with real cowboys, horses, mountains and forests, and could hardly wait to explore the possibilities. What better way to start than to spend some time at a remote cattle ranch? I found an advertisement for a dude ranch that turned out to be a large, working ranch in a beautiful, isolated valley. The owner, a small, hard man named Jack, had a bunch of children who lived in a bunkhouse not far from the main ranch house where I stayed. Because there were no "dudes" around, Jack assigned his two teenage daughters to entertain me. They could not have been more different than the friends I knew growing up. Both were expert riders and herders, spoke with the kind of drawl I had heard only in the movies and seemed totally at home in the wilderness. I was in awe of them.

One day, they invited me to go on a trail ride. I was not quite sure what that meant, but when they brought out a horse for me to ride and proceeded to load up their saddlebags with food and blankets, I assumed it would be an overnight outing on horseback. With help, I mounted the horse and off we went. It was my first time on horseback, my first time in the mountains and the first time I would sleep outdoors. I had complete faith in my companions, however, and was frightened only when my horse began to race through open fields to keep pace with the girls. I hung on for dear life, my heart thundering, as the wind blew through my hair. Hours later, we reached our destination—a forest with old abandoned cabins and corrals scattered under the trees. In the last century, this had been a silver-mining community; when the silver ran out, the cabins were abandoned and the miners moved away.

After helping my friends feed the horses, I limped along behind them as they gathered firewood. We sat on blankets around the fire and cooked dinner. The girls showed me how to put a hot dog on a stick and roast it in the fire. They pulled a couple of cans of corn and beans from their saddlebags, opened them, and we took turns eating right from the can with our spoons.

Suddenly, we heard the shriek of a wild animal echoing through the forest. One of the girls placed her hand on her hip, as if by second nature, feeling for her gun. That evening was the highlight of my youth. It was the kind of adventure I had longed for on those afternoons I spent in Grand Central Station watching the destination board. *Oh, if my friends could only see me now,* I thought to myself. *Eating corn and beans from a can around a campfire, a wild beast crying out in the distance and my friend reaching for her gun.*

That night, we slept wrapped in blankets around the smoldering embers, under a sky teeming with stars. After a breakfast of oranges and coffee, the girls saddled up the horses and we rode back to the ranch. On the way, we passed the Moffat Tunnel, a railroad tunnel through the Continental Divide. As we approached, a troop train filled with young soldiers was just emerging. They leaned out the windows of the train, shouting at the three of us, "Ride 'em, cowboy!" Our horses reared up, just like in the movies. Barely able to hang on to the reins, I raised my borrowed cowboy hat and shouted back, "Howdy, boys!"

At Fitzsimmons Hospital, I made friends with another employee, an older woman. We often chatted about books, politics and the war. One day, she made a comment that changed my life.

"Olga," she said, "you're smart. Have you ever thought about going to college?" The possibility had never crossed my mind. No one in my family or circle of friends had attended college and I was not sure what it entailed. But I was intrigued by the idea. Was I really smart? Was I college material? At 20, was I too old to start? My brother was returning from the Philippines after several years in the Army and he was eager to see our family reunited, so I headed home for a visit. I intended to find out while I was there if college was remotely feasible.

In 1945, I took the entrance examination for Columbia University, scored well and was accepted for admission. I had no idea how I would pay for college, but after more than three years on my own, I was determined not to seek help from my parents. They were struggling to rebuild the house in Westchester County and I knew it would be difficult for them to help me financially. Those were the days before student loans were readily available, so I embarked on a new career as a waitress and temporary office assistant. Working nights, weekends and holidays, I managed to cobble together enough to pay my tuition, with a little extra for spending money.

I lived at home and commuted by subway from the Bronx to the campus at Morningside Heights. The classes were enjoyable and stimulating, but I felt I was missing a "real college experience" by not living on a campus.

After a year at Columbia, I transferred to Ohio University in the small town of Athens and moved into a dormitory with other young women. I worked as a waitress in the afternoons when classes were over, and on Saturday and Sunday. The usual tip was 10 cents. When the time came to pay my tuition, I would march to the bursar's office and pay my expenses dime by dime. Sometimes, it was embarrassing to wait on my friends and their parents who were visiting from out of town, but I knew what I wanted, and a little embarrassment wasn't going to stand in my way.

If waitressing had been a course at Ohio University, I would have flunked. I was clumsy and forgetful, probably because when I wasn't waiting on customers, I was studying at the back of the restaurant. The all-time low of my career as a waitress came when I dropped a soft-boiled egg on a customer's head. He was a good sport about his eggy head of hair and I was grateful that he didn't complain to the management.

Occasionally, a boy I was dating picked me up at the restaurant after work. I would quickly remove my little apron and the ridiculous thing they made us wear on our head, and, still in my waitress uniform, we would head for a coffee shop and hang out until the 10 pm curfew at the dormitory, Lindley Hall.

One evening, shortly before the restaurant was about to close, I was sitting at the end of the counter studying for a test when a traveling salesman came in. I was hoping I could leave early and was a bit grumpy. He sat down at one of the tables and ordered a steak and a beer. After some time, I brought it to him, but the steak was overcooked and I served the wrong brand of beer. He didn't complain. When I gave him the check, he asked if I was studying at the college in town, what I was majoring in and how many hours I worked. I answered his questions, and he said goodbye and left. As I cleared the table, I was astonished to find a one dollar bill under the rim of his plate. It was a substantial amount of money, more than I sometimes earned in an entire evening. I cherish the memory of that encounter—

the empathy that tired traveling salesman showed to an equally tired, struggling college student has stayed with me over the years. To this day, I am a generous tipper.

I was a notorious crammer before exams and sometimes stayed up all night studying. When my roommates and I got hungry, we threw a coat over our pajamas and sneaked out the back door to an all-night diner down the street. After scarfing down a hamburger, we would run back to the dorm with our pajama bottoms rolling down under our coats.

Campus life was fun, but I realized I wasn't learning much at Ohio University. Some of the classes were not even as challenging as those I had taken in high school, so I decided to give Columbia another try. I returned to New York and resumed my studies there, taking a heavy course load so I could graduate in three years. I received a bachelor's degree in political science in 1949, graduating *cum laude*. My diploma was signed by General Dwight D. Eisenhower, the World War II hero who served briefly as president of Columbia before he became President of the United States in 1953.

Shortly after graduation, I applied for a job at the State Department. I longed for a career that would take me to distant places. Following an intense FBI investigation, my application was rejected. It was the first serious disappointment and rejection of my life. There was no explanation. Flaming mad that no one would tell me why I had been turned down, I decided to find out for myself.

I traveled to Washington, D.C. and contacted a classmate from Columbia who was working for the State Department. He told me that because I had been born behind the Iron Curtain and still had relatives living there, someone in the chain of command was concerned that I could be blackmailed. Those were the years of the Red Scare, famously endorsed by Senator Joseph McCarthy, and any connection to someone living behind the Iron Curtain was regarded with suspicion. Such people were viewed as susceptible to pressure.

This seemed to me to be a rational explanation for my rejection. Though my dream of working at the State Department was dashed, I was determined not to go back to New York. It was an exciting time to be living in Washington, as Cold War tensions were mounting in the United States and abroad.

I answered an ad in *The Washington Post* and landed a job working for Drew Pearson, the famed muckraking political columnist. His column, the *Washington Merry-Go-Round*, appeared in hundreds of newspapers nationwide. By attacking hypocrisy, corruption and ineptitude wherever he found it (and sometimes where he didn't), he managed to infuriate just about everyone in Washington, including Senator McCarthy.

A large number of letters from his readers arrived every day. It was my job to answer them, signing my boss's name. They ranged from adoring fan mail to threats, tips, anecdotes, complaints and requests for help. One day, the huge pile of mail included a thin, almost transparent, dime-store envelope with a return address embossed by a cheap hand-held device. It contained a flimsy sheet of paper, at the top of which appeared the name—Albert Einstein. The question of whether to develop the hydrogen bomb was a subject of public discourse at the time, and Pearson had asked the scientist's opinion. Einstein's response was short and to the point. He explained that his opposition to the development of the bomb was well known. Ever since, I have resisted ordering stationery printed with my name— if hand embossing was good enough for Albert Einstein, it's good enough for me.

As a political science major just out of college, I loved being in the middle of the circus that surrounded the Pearson office. The mood was intense. Reporters ran in with the latest scoop and anonymous tips were whispered over the telephone. In the midst of it all, Pearson wrote his daily column, banging away with his two index fingers on a typewriter so ancient that it belonged in a museum. Our office was in a cottage attached to the Pearson pre–Civil War residence on the corner of Dumbarton and N Street in Georgetown. We joked that the building was probably the former slave quarters.

What I liked best about the job was my role as a one-woman social-service agency. I was able to cut through government red tape to get information and results for ordinary citizens who were powerless against the vast bureaucracy. Mrs. X from Keokuk would write complaining that she had not received her social security checks and had tried unsuccessfully for months to get a response from the government. I would pick up the phone and say, "I'm calling for Drew Pearson. Why hasn't Mrs. X received her social security payments?" Those words got immediate attention at the other end of the line.

Within a couple of hours, I'd have a response that Mrs. X might not have received in a year. During the Korean War, I helped to write a weekly column called *GI Gripes* that addressed complaints from servicemen, ranging from objections to the luxuries enjoyed by the top brass to grumblings about the slow delivery of mail from home to the front lines.

I had great respect for my boss and enjoyed my job, but after a couple of years, I realized that it was just that—a job. It was not a calling to which I could commit myself wholeheartedly. I needed to do something more fulfilling with my life—but what?

After a good deal of thought, I came to the realization that the ideal path would be to find work that was intellectually stimulating and would enable me to fight against some of the injustices I saw in the world around me. This was 1951, right at the brink of the civil rights movement. American society was steeped in discrimination against minorities, particularly blacks. It was almost considered the norm, but I had had a few personal encounters with bigotry that had left a deep impression on me.

I was raised by liberal, open-minded parents with a strong sense of social justice. When I was a teenager, my father hired an openly gay carpenter. The shop owners in the area expressed displeasure, but my father responded, "Why should I care what somebody else does in bed? I hired him because he is a good worker. He stays!"

Several years later, when I was returning to the Bronx from Los Angeles on a Greyhound bus, I had a disturbing experience that had a profound impact on me. The bus stopped for a break at a small town in Mississippi and I wandered down the street to see what there was to see. As I strolled along, I noticed an elderly black man, ramrod straight, with a shock of gray hair, walking toward me. I stopped to ask him a question, and to my dismay, he stepped into the gutter to reply so he would be standing at a lower level than me. I was stunned. How could it be that a black gentleman in his 60s felt it necessary to kowtow to a wet-behind-the-ears 17 year-old?

For me, that experience symbolized the rampant racism that was everywhere, including my college town of Athens, Ohio. In 1947, when the Cold War was heating up and McCarthyism was on the horizon, I joined a handful of other students to try to break the color barrier at the restaurants in town. A professor recruited us to call on local restaurants to ask the owners why they would not allow the few black students at the university to dine there. They told us they had no objection, but their customers would not stand for it. So we went through the town, clipboards in hand, ringing doorbells and asking residents if they would object if a black person patronized the restaurants in town. We hadn't gotten very far before the professor was fired. Rumor had it that the administration viewed him as too radical. Our campaign to desegregate the local restaurants ended there.

And now I was working for America's top muckraking columnist who exposed injustice and wrongdoing, both in and out of government. I decided to pursue a career in the law because it would bring me closest to my aspirations of promoting social justice. And with that, I applied to law school. At the time, many law schools would not accept women as students, and there were few females in the legal profession. But I had never let gender stop me before. My father's life showed us that we could have unthinkable dreams and somehow manage to achieve them. My strong, determined parents were not well-educated, but they passed down to us the conviction that anything was possible if you wanted it badly enough and were willing to work for it.

I applied to the School of Law at George Washington University and was admitted. It was a gamble, I knew. The widespread perception that the law was not a suitable occupation for a woman meant that I might not find a job after graduation, but I decided to take the chance. When I told Pearson about my decision, he was supportive, even encouraging. He urged me to continue working for him, pointing out that I could answer his fan mail any time of the day or night, working around my course schedule. I began law school in 1951, working early in the mornings and late at night at the Pearson office.

Even though I could barely pay my tuition and living expenses, I continued to dream of traveling to Europe and decided to take a semester off to make the trip. Saving every penny I could, I often walked to and from work and school through Rock Creek Park for an hour to save the bus fare. Within months, I managed to save enough to buy passage to Europe on a freighter to Hamburg, with several hundred dollars extra for travel. And then, the most extraordinary thing happened.

CHAPTER SIX

SETTLING DOWN: MARRIAGE AND CAREER

I fell in love! During my second year of law school, when I was returning by train to Washington after a visit with my parents in New York, a tall, good-looking man sat down next to me and started a conversation. I was trying to study for a test the next day, but I found him so intriguing that I closed my book and we chatted for the remainder of the trip. The handsome stranger's name was Judd Murray. He was from Seattle, 32 years old, the father of two little boys and recently divorced. I had never met anyone like him.

The boys I had dated previously were either college students or young working men—perfectly nice, but nothing like this dashing, supremely witty, hugely sophisticated man of the world. Judd had run away to sea at the age of 16, joined the Seattle Police Department at 20, married, had two young sons and served as a bomber pilot during World War II. After the war, he returned to Seattle to attend college and continue his work as a police officer.

We arrived in Washington at midnight and he dropped me off by taxi on his way home. When he called me a few days later at the Pearson office, I hesitated. I felt that he was too worldly and too old—six years my senior—but I finally agreed to a date. Unsettled and depressed about the separation from his two young sons, he could not decide whether to remain in Washington or move back to the West Coast to be closer to them.

We saw each other frequently over several months and had many intense conversations about our lives and our relationship. In the end, we decided we were both too unsure about our course in life to make any commitments. Judd moved to San Francisco, and I took a semester off from school and a leave of absence from my job to travel to Europe.

I managed to stretch my meager savings of a few hundred dollars to last for five months on the road. It was unusual for a woman to travel alone in the 1950s, but I always thought that people would be nice to me, and they were. I was a "couch-surfer" before the term was invented. I loved traveling in Europe and could have stayed forever, but I was drawn back by reality. I had just turned 26. If I was going to pursue a career in the law, I needed to get back to the States to finish my last year of law school.

Judd and I continued our long-distance relationship, and he occasionally visited me in Washington. Three years after we met, I decided to move to San Francisco after graduation so we could spend more time together and make a decision about our future.

I graduated in 1954 and made the move to San Francisco. My biggest challenge now was to pass the California Bar Examination. I settled into the Evangeline Residence, a home for girls run by the Salvation Army in a run-down area of the city. It was created to provide safe living quarters for innocent young girls coming to the wicked city from small towns and rural areas. Judd called it "The Home for Unwed Mothers." For $17 a week, I had a small, bright room and two meals a day.

It was a perfect place to study: quiet, clean and safe. I took the examination in August 1954, and to my great relief, I was notified in December that I had passed. Soon after, I joined several hundred other successful candidates to be sworn in by the entire bench of the Supreme Court as a member of the California Bar. Only six women were sworn in that day. After the ceremony, the six of us lined up in the chambers of Chief Justice Phil Gibson for a photo op so that the readers of San Francisco newspapers could see a picture of this exotic species—women lawyers.

To celebrate my admission to the Bar, I headed up to the mountains. I had $83.25 to my name and decided to blow $82.95 on a learn-to-ski-week. After all, I reasoned, I would soon be earning a salary as a lawyer. Five minutes after hitting the slopes, I fell and broke my ankle. I returned to San Francisco by train, in a wheelchair, carrying my ski boots and a pair of crutches in my lap. Even though I was completely broke, I was determined not to ask my family to bail me out. They were still struggling to complete the house in Westchester, and I knew that even though they were strapped, they would not refuse to help me. I explained to the Salvation Army colonel in charge of the Evangeline Residence that I had no money and was unable to look for a job, and she agreed to allow me to stay on until I found work. An orthopedic surgeon took pity on me as well and treated my broken ankle, charging only $10 as his fee.

Holed up in my room for the next two months, I tried to figure out what to do next. There were only a few women in my class at law school and we spoke frequently, and sometimes fearfully, about the prospect of job hunting after graduation. We knew it would be a difficult, possibly humiliating experience. If a woman graduate even managed to get an interview at a law firm, she was often asked if she could type or do secretarial work. The interviewer would explain that clients might object if a woman was assigned to handle their cases and judges would not respect her in court. Even Sandra Day O'Connor, a brilliant graduate of Stanford Law School and the first female United States Supreme Court justice, was asked by a prospective employer if she could type. Job prospects were poor for a woman lawyer and even worse for one on crutches.

I was restless and felt a growing sense of urgency. My career was not moving ahead as planned. Knowing that a whole new batch of potential job applicants was preparing to take the Bar Exam, I wanted to get in the door for an interview before they entered the job market. It was not clear to me how to present myself professionally while hobbling around on crutches. I didn't know if I could even get to an interview.

Then I remembered that the California Supreme Court, housed in the State Building where I had been sworn into the Bar several months earlier, was only two blocks from the Evangeline Residence. I figured I could probably make it that far on crutches. Limping my way down McAllister Street, I struggled up the seven steps to the lobby of the State Building and waited under one of the three arched entryways until a stranger came by and held the door open for me. I hobbled into the office of the Clerk of the Court and approached a man standing at the counter. He happened to be William Sullivan, the Court's chief administrator.

"I came to see if there are any jobs available," I said timidly. He just stared at me. I could only imagine what he was thinking. A skinny little woman hanging onto crutches must have been quite a sight. Overcoming my fear, I continued. "You see, I just passed the Bar Exam and then I broke my leg. So I haven't been able to look for a job. Since I'm staying right down the street, I thought I would come in and ask."

He patiently explained that the only jobs available at the Supreme Court for new law school graduates were as research attorneys (commonly referred to as law clerks) for an individual justice. These jobs were normally arranged far in advance between the justices and top graduates.

The job of a law clerk is one of the most desirable and prestigious positions for a new lawyer and is reserved for the most talented graduates. A newly-minted attorney has the opportunity to learn about the law under the guidance of a wise and experienced judge, and deepen her understanding of legal issues by researching cases and drafting opinions on the judge's behalf. Mr. Sullivan explained that these jobs were in great demand, and, of course, there were no openings. As I turned to leave, he asked me, almost as an afterthought, and probably out of pity, if I would like to leave my résumé.

I hobbled back to the Evangeline Residence, discouraged and frustrated. Several weeks later, the phone rang in my little room. It was Mr. Sullivan. "The chief justice wants to see you at 2:30 tomorrow afternoon in his chambers. Can you be there?"

The next day, I walked into the chambers of Chief Justice Phil Gibson, the same judge who had sworn me in as a member of the California Bar not long before. A law clerk's job for a new graduate typically lasted for one year following graduation or completion of the Bar Exam, but one of the Chief's young staff members had left for Europe before the year was up, and the Justice was looking for a replacement. After an extensive interview, he told me that I would do and offered me the job.

The Chief was a hard taskmaster. His public demeanor was stern and forbidding. Lawyers who argued before the Court and many lower court judges in the state regarded him with apprehension. We, the young lawyers on his staff, were both in awe and terrified at first, but it wasn't long before we realized that the Chief was a marshmallow at heart.

My own realization of his kindness and wisdom came early in my employment, when I was called to his chambers to discuss an opinion I had drafted for him. The sight of the Chief pacing back and forth, his hands clasped behind him, and with a troubled expression on his face, only heightened my anxiety. He began to question me about the basis for some of the statements in the draft opinion and the language I had used to express the conclusions. My face must have reflected the terror I felt because after a few minutes he stopped pacing. He walked over to me and said, "Darlin," (he was from Missouri and addressed all women like this), "if you are going to work with me, you need to understand one thing. If I seem angry, it's because I am trying to get to the bottom of a problem and I am frustrated because I can't find the solution. It has nothing to do with you personally. If I didn't love you, you wouldn't be here!"

That was the last time I felt intimidated by the Chief. Although he was all business at work, he treated his staff almost like family. Away from the Court, he was gracious, funny and warm. Occasionally, he invited us to lunch at some old San Francisco restaurant—a lunch that might last for three or four hours, with drinks flowing freely and lots of interesting talk about life and politics. Once, he asked us to join him at one of the most exclusive men's clubs in San Francisco. He introduced us to his friends there, acting like the proud father of successful adult children.

The Chief demanded clarity and brevity in his opinions, stressing that the purpose was to provide guidance to the lower courts and lawyers. We worked for days and weeks to achieve this, often at staff conferences that he presided over for many hours. At the time, I thought he was somewhat obsessive, but when I look back on those opinions written more than half a century ago, I appreciate his insistence on clear, precise language.

Those were the years when the California Supreme Court was a pioneer in many areas of the law and developed new doctrines that were adopted by the high courts in other states. The atmosphere was heady with intellectual fervor. The staffs and justices were constantly trying to persuade each other to their point of view, or arguing for changes in the language or holdings of pending opinions—all without rancor.

I loved my job. When the Chief asked me to stay on as a member of his permanent staff, I readily agreed.

Judd and I were married by a justice of the peace in July 1955, a few months after I went to work for the Court. The '50s were a fascinating time in San Francisco, with the Beat generation in full bloom. Artists, poets and eccentrics abounded. Life in the city was still quite inexpensive and we managed fairly well, although Judd didn't earn much from his advertising job and my salary at the court was only $275 a month. We paid $100 in rent for a rather run-down apartment with a magnificent view of the city and the bay. It was furnished in a decidedly funky manner, which Judd called "early American landlord." We had a host of friends.

On Friday nights, we went out on the town. Our budget was $5 for the evening for both of us. First, drinks at the Iron Pot, an artists' hangout owned by a warm and funny Italian working-class Italian family. While we chatted with friends, Judd would have two drinks for $1, and I would have one for 50 cents. Then a short walk to Chinatown, where a full dinner, from soup to fortune cookies, cost $1 for each of us. After dinner, we strolled over to the City Lights bookstore in North Beach, a center for the Beat generation and revolutionary ideas. There were a few chairs and tables in the basement, along with a coffeepot and piles of interesting books. We sat engrossed in the eclectic collection of Beat and anarchist literature while we sipped our coffee (25 cents each), until the store closed at midnight. On the few occasions when we bought a book, the cashier seemed almost apologetic, assuring us that it was not necessary to actually purchase one. With the $1 we had left, we walked back to the Iron Pot for an after-dinner drink, before calling it a night.

We went backpacking, skiing or sailing on the bay on a friend's boat on the weekends. Judd was a superb athlete and a patient teacher. Although I was a klutz and never able to do even passably well at any of these activities, I enjoyed getting out on the bay and hiking in the mountains.

In spite of his talent, smarts and charm, Judd could not find a satisfactory niche in life. If there was ever a man who felt out of place working in an office and tied down to a desk, it was Judd Murray. He was too restless and unconventional, and he missed the excitement he had experienced as a young policeman and later as a pilot during the war. Somehow, he had drifted into a career in "point of sale" advertising—designing displays for products at the stores where they were sold. The creative aspects of the work interested him, but when it came time to sell what he had designed, he was inexplicably unsuccessful. It was always a mystery to me. No one I knew had a better gift of gab. He was friendly, smart, funny and outgoing. Yet these qualities did not translate into success when it came to selling the advertising products he designed.

As the years passed and success eluded him, Judd slipped into a downward spiral of drinking and depression. He often talked of changing course—of finding some kind of work that did not confine him to an office and did not require him to rely on the goodwill of others to succeed. But he seemed unable to settle on a path forward. In 1961, after years of tension and failed attempts to work things out, I filed for divorce. It was a traumatic and depressing time for both of us.

I decided to leave San Francisco for some place far, far away where I could start a new life and leave behind the memories of my failed marriage. I had a close friend whose sister and brother-in-law, Jean and George Rogers, were prominent, long-time Alaska residents. "Come on up," they told me, "there are lots of opportunities for lawyers here." I flew to Juneau, where the Rogers lived in a pretty wooden house they had built on a hill overlooking the sea after they first arrived in Alaska in 1945.

George arranged for me to meet the state's Attorney General. On a snowy, freezing afternoon, I was ushered into a warm, cozy, but somewhat chaotic office, where Alaska's Attorney General was sitting in a comfortable chair, with his sleeves rolled up and his feet propped on a wood stove. I was taken aback. This was nothing like the stately chambers of the California Supreme Court, where the staff and the judges dressed formally and kept their feet firmly on the floor.

After asking about my experience, the Attorney General told me that if I came to work for his office, I could specialize in any area of law I chose. He explained that since Alaska had only recently achieved statehood, the judicial system was in the process of development and there were many jobs for lawyers. The field was wide open and there was a good likelihood that I would be appointed a judge if I performed well at his office. "There's only one thing," he said. "We need a letter from your employer stating that you are a member in good standing of the Bar and that your work at the court has been satisfactory."

When I returned to San Francisco, I told the Chief about my divorce, my visit to Alaska and the job offer, contingent on a recommendation from him. To my consternation, he responded, "I'm not going to do it." He sat me down and gave me a long—but sympathetic—lecture about running away from problems instead of facing them bravely. He urged me to stay on at the Court. I was confused, unsure what to do. I knew that the path I chose would impact the rest of my life. I loved San Francisco, my work at the Court, my colleagues, and I had many friends who were close to my heart. In the end, I decided to stay.

The chief retired in 1964, and I joined the staff of Associate Justice Stanley Mosk, who was appointed to the Court that year. He had been the youngest trial-court judge in California and came to the Supreme Court after several years as the state's Attorney General. A political liberal, he famously described the radical John Birch Society as a cadre of "wealthy businessmen, retired military officers and little old ladies in tennis shoes." Justice Mosk had a great sense of humor and a gentle but firm manner. I felt fortunate to be a member of his staff.

One afternoon, I ran into my friend Alice, a staff attorney for another justice. We were hurrying down the wide, carpeted hallway to the chambers of our respective judges to discuss the opinions we were working on with them. For a moment, we talked about some personal matters, and then, as we parted, Alice turned around and said, "Can you believe we're getting paid for this?"

That summed it up! I felt I had the best job in the law. I worked with the smartest people, most of them refugees from private practice. We worked carefully and had high principles, and though we argued frequently and heatedly over cases, we were friends. As more women entered the legal profession over the years, I had a few job offers, but decided to make the Court my life's work. I ended up staying for 37 years. During that time, I helped to write important decisions in the areas of civil rights, women's rights and environmental policy.

Ironically, Judd went off to Alaska to become a commercial fisherman after our divorce. He had been around boats all his life from the time he was born on a houseboat at the base of a fjord in British Columbia, where his father ran a lumber camp. As an expert seaman and navigator, the life of a commercial fisherman, with all its excitement and physical demands, suited him well. He fished for crab in the frigid waters of Alaska and returned to the Bay Area each year after the fishing season was over.

Despite our divorce, or maybe because of it, Judd and I remained devoted to one another until his death in 1976. A wonderful gift from my marriage was the bond I developed with his two sons, Pat and Steve, Pat's partner Beth and Steve's wife Fermina, my grandchildren Sean and Colin, and Danielle and Suzanne, the spectacular women they married. We remain close to this day.

Painting of our little cottage in Transylvania

Passport photo, 1931, with my mother, my brother Alex, and sisters Shirley and Bertha. I am on the lower right.

Family photo sent to my father when he was in America

Our family in Crotona Park in the Bronx

My father, Joseph

My mother, Matilda

With Bertha, my little sister

Alex and my mother

My father and his beloved cello

A teenager growing up in New York

Matilda and Joseph Davis in their 70s

A student at Ohio University

Passport photo, 1952

Marriage to Judd Murray, July 30, 1955

Backpacking trip with
Judd and our friend, Jack

Together in Hawaii

Sailing in Canada

Skiing with Judd and my
stepsons, Pat and Steve

Chief Justice Phil Gibson,
my first boss at the
California Supreme
Court

Associate Justice Stanley Mosk, my boss for
twenty-eight years at the California Supreme Court

CHAPTER SEVEN

CHILDREN OF A LESSER GOD

Eight years after Judd's death, I found myself being carried in a basket by a porter through the Himalayas, my left leg wrapped in a dark green plastic garbage bag. When my fellow trekkers and I finally reached Kathmandu, I consulted Dr. Ashok Banskota, a young Nepali orthopedic surgeon about my injury. It was a lucky call. Not only did he treat my injured leg, but through him, Allan and I learned about the desperate plight of children with disabilities in Nepal. This led to the creation of one of the largest scholarship programs in the country for disabled children.

Dr. Banskota recommended that I get an x-ray of my leg and directed me to a storefront establishment in a rundown neighborhood. When I arrived, I found two sleepy young men lounging inside a dusty office. I explained my mission and they escorted me into a small room, threw a shield over my leg and revved up a creaky old machine. After a couple of minutes, one of them came rushing in shouting, "It's broken, it's broken!" Like the old Nepali hand I was becoming, I assumed he was referring to the x-ray machine. "Okay, I'll come back tomorrow," I replied. He looked puzzled and shouted even louder, "It's the leg, the leg!"

He placed the x-ray film in an envelope and instructed a taxi driver to take me to the small medical center where Dr. Banskota worked. The operating room was on the third floor and there was no elevator. I had two choices: I could try to find someone to carry me, or I could shimmy up backward, step-by-step, on my butt, in my tight jeans. I'd had enough of riding around on the backs of strangers and decided to climb up under my own steam. Dr. Banskota set my leg in a plaster cast and provided me with loose pajama bottoms for the journey back to my hotel.

After I returned to California, I was fitted with a comfortable fiberglass cast that snapped off for bathing. My leg healed quickly.

When I asked my doctor what I should do with the cast, he said, "Throw it away." But by then I had an inkling of how valuable some things are in Asia that we take for granted in the States and decided to take the cast with me when I returned to Nepal. Perhaps Dr. Banskota could use it for one of his patients.

As soon as I reached Kathmandu the following year, I tracked down Dr. Banskota. I found him at a 32 bed orthopedic hospital for children that he had recently opened in the Jorpati section of Kathmandu. He had been trained abroad and could easily have practiced in the West, but chose to return to Nepal to care for children with disabilities. Dr. Banskota was one of the few orthopedic surgeons in the country. In fact, his hospital was the first of its kind in Nepal, and desperately needed. Treatment was free for a large majority of patients, almost all of whom came from impoverished families.

Nepal was awash with disabled children. Few had received medical care of any kind, in part because they were stigmatized by society. There was a widespread belief that a disability is punishment for sins committed by the child or the parent in a prior life, so there was little incentive to interfere with what they viewed as a child's destiny. A large proportion of the disabled population was illiterate. Without an education, they were relegated to the most barren lives, unable to earn a living. The plight of disabled girls was particularly desperate because many of them never marry, remaining a life-long burden to their families.

When I visited the hospital, I was deeply touched by the children I saw there. Some of them languished at the hospital for months, even years, if they needed long-term care or their parents did not return to retrieve them. They had nothing much to occupy them during the day, so I asked Dr. Banskota if I could come to the hospital to play with them. Three mornings a week, I hung out with the children in the sunny courtyard when they were not undergoing medical procedures. We joked, teased each other and played games, sometimes with borrowed toys.

Day after day, I saw children with terrible disabilities arriving at the hospital, often carried for long distances in a basket over mountain trails to get to the nearest road. They were accompanied by dazed relatives, many of whom had never left their villages before, and had never seen a vehicle or an electric light. Some children had limbs crippled by polio or terrible scars from burns incurred years earlier. Others had simply been abandoned at the hospital by families too poor to feed another mouth. The devotion and skill of the staff, and the sweetness, earnestness and beauty of the children amazed me. Against all odds, it was a happy place.

One day, Dr. Banskota invited me into his office and introduced me to Tara, a pretty 11 year-old girl. She was sitting on his examination table, dangling her legs over the side. The doctor asked her to lift her long skirt and I was astounded to see that she had two artificial legs. They had been burned off in a fire, and until two years before, she could only crawl. Dr. Banskota performed an operation and fitted her with artificial limbs. Now, she proudly walked across the room as the doctor and I looked on. He remarked that when Tara returned to her village, she would not be able to walk to school because of the rough terrain, and asked if I knew someone she could live with in Kathmandu so she could attend school. "I don't know anyone," I replied, "but I can send her to boarding school."

That opened the floodgates. When the hospital staff learned that Tara had received a scholarship to boarding school in Kathmandu, they showered me with heart-rending stories about all the little geniuses discharged from the hospital who would never get an education unless Allan and I helped them.

We talked it over and decided to expand our scholarship program to support disabled children, including those who were blind and deaf. Shortly thereafter, we sponsored the education of three other disabled girls recommended by the hospital, two of them blind.

We were able to help these children, but there were some whose medical problems were too challenging to be addressed in Nepal.

The first of these was Anjita. To my dying day, I will remember my first glimpse of her one morning when I was playing with the children at Dr. Banskota's hospital. She was a wisp of a child, with a dreadfully scarred little face. One eye was burned shut and she was mostly bald, with a huge blister running from her bare scalp to the place where her nose should have been. What was most astonishing about her though, was the joy that radiated from her as she played with the other little patients, her tinkly laugh echoing around the room. She was seemingly unaware of her unusual appearance and the other children couldn't have cared less.

This tiny, eight-year-old, 35 pound bundle of high spirits intrigued me. Dr. Banskota told me that when Anjita was only a few months old, she had rolled into a cooking fire on the floor of her family hut and suffered severe burns to her face and one hand. Her mother sold the gold that had been her dowry—the entire family capital—to correct the terrible consequences of the accident. However, there was no trained plastic surgeon in Nepal at the time, and the results of several surgeries were not encouraging. The huge bubble that concealed part of Anjita's face was the result of an attempt by a surgeon to construct a nose, using skin from her scalp.

I could not get Anjita out of my mind. Shortly after I met her, a medical team from Interplast, an American nonprofit organization, traveled to Nepal to perform surgery for children with cleft palates and other conditions. We took Anjita for a consultation, but of course they were unable to help a child with such extensive damage. One of the doctors suggested that we contact Shriners Hospital for Children in San Francisco, explaining that although it was largely devoted to treating children with orthopedic problems, the hospital also provided reconstructive surgery for children with serious burns. For those who qualified, care was free.

Dr. Bob Gilbert, a good friend and prominent orthopedic surgeon, was on the board of the hospital and I asked him if it would be possible to admit Anjita. After months of discussion, the hospital agreed that it might accept her if, after a personal consultation, the surgeons determined they could help her.

This led to a flurry of activity to obtain a visa for Anjita: visits to doctors for physical exams and vaccinations, detailed documentation of her background and family, and securing a Nepali passport. In early February 1993, we boarded a Singapore Airlines plane bound for San Francisco, with a two-day stop in Singapore on the way. Anjita's entire family—her parents and five sisters—were there to give her a send-off, all shedding copious tears. Not Anjita. She kissed each of them briskly, told her pretty sister Binu that she would look just like her when she returned and marched into the airport without looking back. Anjita was not the only child who boarded the plane with me that day.

Paru, a Nepali girl in our scholarship program, was also a candidate for treatment at Shriners Hospital. She was 16 years old, slight of build, beautiful, and suffering from a severe orthopedic disability. Her right leg was six inches shorter than her left. The entire leg was encased in a heavy brace that reached to her hip, with her foot strapped onto a high platform. She was able to walk, but with great difficulty. We hoped that Shriners would admit her for a complex leg-lengthening procedure that was unavailable in Nepal.

Paru had lived with her large, impoverished family in a remote village, where she contracted osteomyelitis when she was 18 months old. For four years, she walked for two hours each way to school — barefoot, leaning on a stick, in agony. She received no medical care until she was nine years old, when a stranger came to her village and told her father about the orthopedic hospital in Jorpati. By that time, her right leg had grown into a thin double spiral that was much shorter than her left. Dr. Banskota managed to straighten out the leg in a series of operations, but he was unable to lengthen it to coincide with her left leg. Paru spent years in the hospital, alone, often in pain. After her discharge at the age of 12, we gave her a scholarship to attend boarding school.

Paru and Anjita had never seen a tall building or used a western toilet. In Nepal, it is customary to eat with your hands, and they had never eaten with utensils. On the plane, the girls took it all in stride and carefully mimicked my every move as I unlatched the tray table, unwrapped my napkin and used my knife and fork. By the end of the journey, their table manners were impeccable. When we arrived at the airport in San Francisco, we were greeted by a group of my close friends waving welcome signs and colorful balloons.

The plan was for the two girls to live with my long-time friends, Joanne and Tot Heffelfinger, who had a large house and an empty nest. They had raised six children and were grandparents several times over, but they did not hesitate to open their home and their hearts to Anjita and Paru. Once again, Joanne and Tot cheerfully embraced the burdens of parenthood, chauffeuring the kids everywhere and providing them with the most loving care and attention. Their days and years were taken up with medical appointments, hospital visits and other parental duties.

Since I would be in the States for several months before returning to Nepal, we decided that Anjita would stay with me until my departure in the fall. And so, at the age of 67, I embarked on a new adventure—full-time motherhood. My stepsons Pat and Steve were 10 and 12 years old when I married Judd, and they had lived with us only during school vacations.

On her first visit to Shriners Hospital, Anjita met Dr. Angelo Capozzi, the plastic surgeon who would change her life. She needed surgery on virtually her entire face—her left ear and eye, her lips, her nose, her scalp and the scarred skin that covered all but a small portion of her face. At first, Dr. Capozzi seemed overwhelmed by the extent of Anjita's burns, but he decided to begin with a minor operation to release a skin contraction on her forehead. This was the first of multiple surgeries on her face and scalp. Over more than a dozen years, the doctor built a functioning nose, replaced most of the skin on Anjita's face with a graft from her stomach and made many other improvements in her appearance. A mane of thick black hair miraculously sprouted on her little bald head. During most of this time, Anjita's face was seriously disfigured, but she bore the stares and occasional comments bravely. She adored Dr. Capozzi and became his favorite patient in all his decades of practice.

Anjita was a captivating child—stubborn, strong, funny, loving and sometimes exasperating. She was full of fun and mischief, with a grace that was amazing in light of her disfigurement. I learned a great deal from her. Once, when I was angry about something she had done, I shouted at her, wagging my finger in her charred little face. I was ashamed and alarmed by the look of terror in her eyes, almost as though I was beating her mercilessly. I suddenly realized that I was doing something completely unacceptable. It is frightening and humiliating for a Nepali child to be yelled at by someone from another culture. I learned a painful lesson and have never raised my voice since, to her or any of our other children.

The six months that Anjita lived with me turned out to be among the most memorable and enjoyable times of my life. Despite my lack of maternal skills and experience, we managed to establish a close bond and have a great deal of fun. Each evening, after her bath, I would wrap her in a big towel and we would watch an hour of animal shows on television. Then I would carry her to her room, adjacent to mine. Like other Nepali children, she had never slept alone, so I stayed with her until she fell asleep.

Late one night, long after I had put her to bed and was sound asleep in my room, I was awakened by the most heart-rending sobs. I looked down, and there was Anjita sitting on the floor beside my bed, bawling away. "What's the matter?" I asked. She replied with something that sounded like, *"Door lagcha."* I had no idea what she was saying and pleaded with her to return to her bed, but she kept wailing her little refrain over and over again. I turned my back and pretended to sleep, but nothing would stop her lament. After about an hour, I picked her up in my arms and carried her to her room. In a few seconds, she was back, bawling even louder, *"Door lagcha, door lagcha!"*

Finally, in a haze of exhaustion and exasperation, I got out of bed and found my Nepali-English dictionary. Bleary-eyed though I was, I discovered what she had been trying to tell me, "I'm afraid, I'm afraid!" She had awakened in the middle of the night and found herself alone in bed for the first time in her life. The solution was simple. I swooped her up in my arms and we returned to her room. With my arm around her waist as she cuddled close, we both fell asleep immediately, exhausted.

My fellow surrogate mother Joanne and I spent hours at the hospital almost every day and often all night if the girls were undergoing surgery. Anjita and Paru had more visitors than all the other patients combined. Scores of our friends stopped by to bring gifts and sit by their bedsides telling jokes and stories. They adored the girls and accompanied us on outings to playgrounds, the zoo, museums, restaurants, Disneyland and "pickling"—Anjita's word for "picnic."

The extraordinary kindness of strangers as I rambled around town with Anjita and Paru amazed me. At first, people stared at the sight of a white-haired woman shepherding a pint-sized kid with a scarred face and a beautiful teenager with a terrible limp, wearing a long skirt to hide her prosthesis. Then, they often did something overwhelmingly heartwarming to let us know they cared.

I first noticed this on the flight from Kathmandu to Singapore. An elderly Japanese gentleman who was seated several rows behind us walked up the aisle and presented the girls with an intricate origami flower that he had made from a magazine on board. In San Francisco, taxi drivers charged us half what the meter showed, bus drivers allowed us to ride free and strangers approached us on the street to offer help. A couple of times when we were at a restaurant together and I went to pay the bill, the cashier told me that someone had already taken care of it. I remember a shopping trip to a fancy department store where not one but two strangers walked up to Anjita and said, "You're the cutest little girl I've ever seen!"

My favorite encounter with a stranger occurred when Anjita and I were waiting to board a cable car on Market Street in San Francisco. A nice-looking black man tending his shoeshine stand on the corner ran over and offered Anjita a free shoeshine. "Why not?" I thought and we walked a few steps to his stand. Her feet barely reached the footrest. As he snapped his polishing cloth, he kept up a running patter about his own disfigurement as a child due to parental abuse and the many surgeries he had endured as a result. He said that he had overcome his sense of inferiority and embarrassment and gone on to live a happy life. Every few sentences he turned to me, asking me to translate his remarks. My Nepali was wholly inadequate to the task, but Anjita got the drift of what he was saying. When we heard the clang of the approaching cable car, Anjita hopped off the stand, we said a hasty "thank you," and ran for the car. The man followed us and thrust a Giants t-shirt into her hand. "A gift for your father," he said. As the cable car slowly began to climb Nob Hill, Anjita turned around on the outside step, threw her arms around the shoeshine man and they gave each other a great bear hug.

Although Anjita was at ease with adults, most of whom found her irresistible, it was painful for her to meet other children. She seemed to trust only infants and other disabled kids. Anjita had started school in her village in Nepal, but quit after a few months because of the stares and rude comments of the other students. Her response was to make faces at them and get into fistfights—hard to imagine for a kid who weighed less than 35 pounds, but I have no doubt that what she lacked in strength she made up in spirit. When it came time to enroll her in school in the fall, the Heffelfingers, savvy and incisive parents, asked their son Matt to make a video to lay the groundwork for her appearance in class. The film showed her playing with the dog, riding a bike and doing other things a child her age would normally do. The entire student body at the school viewed the video. The California Burn Foundation, as part of its program to integrate children with burns into school, sent a handsome fireman, decked out in his big hat and bulky uniform, to talk to the teachers and students. By the time Anjita attended her first class, all 280 kids in the school wanted to be her friends.

She enjoyed school and made a number of friends. The teachers paid special attention to her needs, tutoring her privately when she was too disfigured by her surgeries to appear in class. Anjita had a flair for language and she learned proper, unaccented English very quickly. Sometimes, she would come home from school and say things like, "C'mere, you guys," or "He's a cool dude." It was hard to keep a straight face when we heard these teenage slang words coming out of her little Nepali mouth.

We were concerned, however, that Anjita refused to look in a mirror. Because mirrors are not a common item in Nepali villages, she had rarely seen her own reflection. She loved pretty clothes and wanted to see how she looked in them, but when we took her shopping, we practically had to cover her face to persuade her to take a peek in the mirror. Gradually, after a few years, this changed as her appearance improved following successive surgeries. She began to look at her reflection, tossing her head of new long black hair and grinning at herself. One day, she called me on the phone and said excitedly, "Olga Mommy, guess what! Joanne Mommy just bought me a new jean jacket and overalls with flowers on them. You should see me. I'm so cute!"

Anjita lived with the Heffelfingers throughout her childhood. They showered her with love and provided her with every advantage a child could possibly wish for. After graduating from a private high school in San Francisco, she attended Mt. Holyoke College. She has returned to Nepal twice and has remained close to her family.

Since college, Anjita has worked with children and adults with special needs. She has an uncanny ability to relate to them. As of this writing, she is working with a 24 year-old man who has the mental capacity of a four-year-old. In the mornings, she teaches him to talk and perform simple tasks. In the afternoons, she takes him on stimulating excursions—out for lunch, hiking, ferry rides and visits with friends. She adores him and talks about him constantly to friends and family; her iPhone is filled with his photos. And he idolizes her. For the first time in his life, he speaks in sentences. His father told Anjita that his son is happier than he has ever been. Anjita has no formal training with special-needs individuals and plans to return to school to enhance her instinctive gift. She has a green card and is on track to becoming an American citizen. And now Anjita has a serious boyfriend; he is an all-American type who is strong, funny, dependable and kind. Joanne and I, her American mothers, are delighted with her choice.

Paru's path in the United States did not go as smoothly as Anjita's. She spent many months in the hospital in great pain. The leg-lengthening procedure was only moderately effective, because new bone growth was hampered as a result of the poor nourishment she had received as a child. She was almost excessively devoted to her studies. At 16, she lagged behind in school because she had spent so much of her childhood in the hospital and her slow academic progress was a source of constant anguish. The Heffelfingers hired a private tutor, but this proved unsatisfactory. We didn't think Paru would do well at the local high school, which was fairly rigorous, because her English was not good enough.

Then, magically, a generous donor offered to pay her way to an excellent boarding school close by that could accommodate her disability and provide her with special tutoring when she was in the hospital. Paru loved the school, did well academically, and was one of the most popular girls in her class. Despite missing months of school, she made the honor role in 9th grade. The wall by her hospital bed was covered with butcher paper bearing scores of notes from her classmates and teachers. Paru was so admired and respected that the school established a prize in her name. The award is given every year to a student at her dormitory who demonstrates the courage, devotion to her studies and good cheer that she exemplified.

Paru returned to Nepal after almost three years in San Francisco. Although she had gained only three and a half inches in the length of her right leg and still required a high platform shoe, her prosthesis was lighter and stronger. She finished high school, graduated from a private college in Kathmandu and went on to receive a master's degree and a doctorate in gender and development studies from the prestigious Asian Institute of Technology in Bangkok. Paru is the Nepal Youth Foundation's first, and so far only, PhD. She works as a specialist on gender-related issues for various international organizations in Nepal.

In 1994, a 10 year-old boy named Ajay joined our family of Nepali children in the United States. He was born with a condition called exstrophy. His intestines were exposed and his bladder was on the outside of his body. Because he could not control his bladder, he wore a urine-soaked towel around his waist at all times. School was out of the question for Ajay, and he lived more or less as an outcast.

His father had died in a landslide, and his mother, pregnant with him at the time, had a mental breakdown. Ajay was not expected to survive, but an uncle rescued him and provided him with food and shelter. When Ajay turned four, the uncle brought him to Kathmandu to seek medical care. He had no idea where to turn and finally sought help from Dr. Banskota. However, since Ajay did not have an orthopedic problem, the doctor referred him to the government hospital. There, he was able to get some help, but the only permanent solution the Nepali doctors could offer was an external pouch that he would have to maintain for the rest of his life.

At Dr. Banskota's suggestion, Allan and I visited Ajay at the rather chaotic government hospital. Medical care was free, but nourishing food, medicine and certain items needed for surgery were not. The uncle had run out of money and Dr. Banskota hoped that we would be able to help.

I will never forget my first sight of Ajay—a small, very thin child, all eyes, his body bristling with tubes and needles, tears running down his cheeks. It was love at first sight for Allan and me, and we visited regularly, bringing food, toys and treats and providing money for necessities. He was particularly delighted with the little cars we brought, which he raced up and down the windowsill next to his bed. At first, he was so shy that he would not even look at us, but we persevered and finally won him over. The first time we saw him smile—a smile that lit up the whole room—we were overjoyed.

When I spoke to the doctor at the government hospital about Ajay, he told us there was a surgical procedure to avoid the necessity for a pouch, but it was not available in Nepal. Once again, I turned to my go-to contact, Dr. Bob Gilbert, and asked if the California Pacific Medical Center, where he practiced, would perform the surgery without cost. It took a lot of work and persuasion on his part, but he was finally able to convince the hospital to admit Ajay for surgery.

I was somewhat apprehensive about taking a child in this condition on a 23 hour flight to the States, with an overnight stop at a hotel in Singapore. But I armed myself with plenty of towels and plastic sheets, and the trip proved to be quite enjoyable and without mishap. Like Anjita and Paru, Ajay had never flown on a plane, stayed in a hotel or eaten western food using utensils, but he carefully watched my every move and seemed to be at ease throughout the trip. He turned out to be a curious and cheerful traveling companion.

In a complex operation, the doctors constructed an internal bladder out of Ajay's own intestines, eliminating the necessity for an external pouch. Following discharge from the hospital, he needed to stay in the States for six months for follow-up. For most of that time, Ajay stayed with my friends Sam Silverman, a veterinarian and his wife, Gloria, who provided him with the most loving, supportive, meticulous care. Beyond this, they did a great job of teaching Ajay the basics of life in America. He learned to bowl, became a Star Trek addict and a devotee of country music. You don't know what culture shock is until you've heard a little Nepali boy belting out "All My Exes Live in Texas."

Ajay spent a considerable amount of time at my house. He passed endless hours satisfying his obsession with Bugs Bunny on television, sometimes laughing so hard that he fell off the couch. When he first arrived, I taught him something all American children need to know—how and when to call 911. I carefully explained that this was to be done only in the most dire emergency, such as a fire. Otherwise, big red fire trucks full of firemen in flashy hats and bulky uniforms would come rushing up to the house within minutes. Five, maybe 10 minutes later, the telephone rang. "Did you call 911?" the operator inquired. When I told her I had not, she asked if someone else in the house could have done so. "Impossible," I replied. "The only other person in the house is a young Nepali child who barely knows how to dial a telephone."

When I questioned Ajay, he gave me a look of complete innocence and denied making the call. For years, I assumed that perhaps I had been too graphic in describing the consequences of calling 911. What little boy could resist the excitement of large red fire trucks filled with firemen carrying hoses, rolling up to the door with their sirens blaring? Many years later, Ajay told me he had been speaking the truth. He had not dialed 911. But he was so homesick that he had randomly pushed a few buttons on the phone in the hopes of reaching his uncle in Nepal.

When Ajay returned to Nepal, he was able to attend school, ride a bike and play soccer, just like any kid his age. He is exceptionally smart and caught up to his grade level quickly. After he graduated from high school in Kathmandu, he went on to law school and is currently practicing law with an excellent firm in Kathmandu.

The following year, I brought Bikash, a young boy who suffered from the same condition as Ajay, to the United States for surgery at the Lucille Packard Children's Hospital at Stanford. Once again, the hospital, doctors and nurses provided care without charge. After a long, difficult operation, Bikash moved into the home of Ed and Sandy Mueller, another pair of empty nesters. During the six months he lived with them, the Muellers virtually gave up their normal lives. For several weeks, Bikash was in a full-body cast, requiring intense care at home. His English was not as good as Ajay's, but he and the Muellers managed well and grew very close. Bikash spent a lot of time fooling around with something he had never seen before: a computer. The Muellers taught him how to use it to play games and learn English. By the time he returned to Nepal, his English was much improved and, like Ajay, he was able to live a normal life. Bikash went to school for the first time, and ultimately graduated from college with a degree in public health. Today, he works at a very good hospital not far from Kathmandu.

In these days of drive-by shootings, public beheadings and ethnic cleansing, I am comforted by the memory of the sweet and generous acts of total strangers while I traveled around San Francisco with Anjita and Paru. I will always remember the empathy, devotion, and sacrifice in time and treasure made by the Heffelfingers, the Silvermans and the Muellers, as well as by the doctors, nurses and hospitals on both continents that provided first-class care without charge. Their compassion and generosity transformed these children from pariahs who would have been shunned by society for their entire lives to successful, cheerful, confident young adults working to improve the world.

When Allan and I gave scholarships to four disabled girls in 1988, we could not have imagined that the program would ultimately become one of the largest in Nepal supporting the education of disabled children, some through college and even beyond. Many graduates have gone on to successful, rewarding careers. Two are serving as high officers in the Nepali government, the first blind employees to achieve such status. A few of the blind high school students hosted weekly radio programs promoting the welfare of the disabled population. Another alumnus, the first blind lawyer in Nepal, won a case in the appellate court with an argument so compelling that it inspired an editorial in Nepal's English-language newspaper, the *Kathmandu Post*. The editorial emphasized the potential of people with disabilities to contribute to society.

One blind graduate summed it up this way, "If I had not gotten a scholarship to boarding school, I would have been a beggar wandering on the streets or I could have even died. I am satisfied with my life. Even if I can't see the material world with my eyes, I can always see the world with the eyes of my education and knowledge. Without an education, I would have been blind both internally and externally."

I grew particularly close to a little blind girl who came from a remote village to attend boarding school in Kathmandu. Shanta had a tremendous desire to learn. Despite her handicap, she became a top student, and received a scholarship to Colorado State University under a U.S. State Department program. She has become a prominent and effective spokesperson for the rights of the disabled in Nepal. Many newspaper articles have been written about her, and she has appeared frequently on television, including a long interview with a talk show host who called himself the Larry King of Nepal.

In 2004, Shanta was the first Nepali athlete to participate in the Paralympic Games in Athens, competing in the shot put and the 100 and 200-meter races. She, along with her blind brother and sister, who were also educated through our scholarship program, are helping to change perceptions of the disabled. As Shanta told an interviewer,

"Now we have proved we are not damaged goods." Shanta is the executive director of the Rose International Fund for Children, a new organization that works for the welfare of people with disabilities in Nepal. She plans to devote her life to the cause.

She occasionally reminds me, "Mom, how lucky I am! I can't imagine what would have become of me if you had not broken your leg!"

CHAPTER EIGHT

NEW BEGINNINGS

As I began spending more time in Nepal, I was overwhelmed by the needs of its children. Allan and I knew we were improving the lives of dozens of kids we happened to come upon, but so many others lived in desperate circumstances, without education, health care, nutritious food or shelter. I realized that if we wanted to make a difference in this ocean of want, we would have to reach out to more children.

During the late '80s, when Allan lived with a Nepali family and I stayed in a Kathmandu hotel, we were pretty much a "mom-and-pop" operation. Our files were stashed in tin trunks under our beds, and we had no office. Those were the days before mobile phones, and Paropakar Orphanage served as our home base, office and meeting place for anyone who wanted to contact us. We camped out there every afternoon when the boys came home from school.

Scholarship funds for Paropakar boys and disabled children had come almost entirely from my own pocket or our circle of friends, who donated generously and without too much arm-twisting. But we knew that if we wanted to help more children, we would have to reach out to the general public for support. The pressure to give scholarships and other aid was very great, and sometimes we couldn't resist desperate pleas for help, even though we were not sure how we would raise the money to pay for it. I often lay awake at night worrying, adding up scholarship figures in my head, to be sure that the obligations we had undertaken did not exceed my personal savings, in the event that some of our donors stopped their support. Ultimately, I concluded that the only way to expand the scope of our fundraising was to form a nonprofit entity that would allow us to seek tax-exempt donations.

In 1989, I began the process. After months of research and contact with federal and state authorities, we launched the Nepalese Youth Opportunity Foundation, later renaming it the Nepal Youth Foundation. In June 1990, the Internal Revenue Service approved our foundation as a tax-exempt public charity—a major milestone. I became the president and Allan the secretary.

Our fledgling foundation faced another obstacle. To succeed, I needed to spend more time working at the new foundation than my demanding job at the California Supreme Court allowed. I was grateful to Justice Mosk, my boss, for allowing me to take extra time off for extended visits to Nepal year after year, but other staff members had to take on additional burdens during my long absences. I knew the situation could not last forever. With a mixture of regret at leaving a job I had found so fulfilling, coupled with excitement at the prospect of a new life, in 1992 I retired from my job at the Supreme Court after 37 years. At the age of 67, I launched into a full-time career as NYF's president and chief fundraiser, spending half the year in Nepal and the rest at my home in Sausalito, California.

As Allan and I came across children desperately in need of care, we searched everywhere for a boarding school that would take all of them. We had collected a motley group of 18 homeless, blind and disabled kids and found housing for them at a temporary shelter. Some of the children were referred to us by Child Workers in Nepal, an organization serving street children. Others came from Dr. Banskota's hospital or were simply left at our doorstep. Surprisingly, they were a cheerful lot, happy to have a roof over their heads and the opportunity to go to school.

With the new school year approaching, we sent the blind children to the Lab School where they could learn Braille and other necessary skills while living with one of the teachers. Shortly after they were settled, two blind youngsters, a brother and sister with mental disabilities, joined the group. They had been abandoned by their family. A stranger had found them begging at a temple and brought them to our doorstep with a clear message to the person who answered the doorbell, "For the two Americans."

It was difficult to find a school that would accept the 12 remaining children, but we finally convinced a boarding school to admit all of them. It wasn't long, however, before we realized that the school was not suitable for our kids. They were subjected to derogatory comments from other students, and the principal compelled them to worship his guru each morning, threatening to cut their food rations if they failed to do so. We didn't want to separate them because they had become a close-knit family and were so attached to each other. Like the boys at Paropakar, the older kids protected the little ones and tried to help with their problems.

But the chance of finding a decent boarding school willing to take them all was slim. The only alternative was to open our own children's home. Allan and I had discussed the possibility, but we always ended up being dead set against the idea. We were both spending only part of the year in Kathmandu, and it didn't seem feasible to run a year-round residence for children from halfway around the world. But unable to come up with any other solution, we reluctantly decided to open a home for boys in Kathmandu in 1992. It turned out to be one of the best decisions we ever made.

We rented a small three-bedroom house and hired a former Paropakar boy and his new wife to be the resident supervisors. They played the role of surrogate parents, providing the children with guidance, support and affection. Within two years, the house was overflowing, so we rented a larger, more comfortable home that was soon filled with 30 boisterous boys. They named their new home J House because of its location in the Jawalakhel district of Patan, in the urban area near Kathmandu.

We were itching to start a home for girls, who were typically the victims of harsh discrimination and neglect in Nepal. They were less likely to be sent to school than boys or to receive proper nourishment or medical care. Many were forced to work from an early age, and some were married off before they were 14 years old. In 1995, we rented a second house for girls near J House and named it K House.

J and K Houses sheltered some of the most vulnerable children in the country: orphans, abandoned and disabled children, beggars, child laborers, street kids and youngsters who had been living behind bars with an incarcerated parent. Some had endured more trauma and suffering from an early age than many of us experience in a lifetime. Each child arrived with a unique, heart-breaking story. What they had in common, however, was a chance to begin a new life—an opportunity to start over as part of the J and K House family.

We met Manish at the dilapidated medieval Central Jail for men in Kathmandu. He was five years old and could not remember a time when he was not behind bars. Manish lived in the jail with his father, who was serving a 20 year sentence. He and a number of other boys at the Central Jail had a similar history. Their fathers were sentenced to prison, their mothers had abandoned them and they had no family willing or able to care for them. The only alternative to jail was living on the street. Inhumane as it sounds, their incarceration represented an act of compassion by the warden, who allowed them to share a cot and the meager rations with their fathers.

Most of the inmates were not confined to locked cells, but lived in open, arched galleries that encircled a crumbling ruin of a building. The walls were lined with newspaper to patch the holes, and the roof was so ancient and leaky that the ceiling was covered with permanent blue plastic sheeting. The prisoners slept on cots lined up close to one another. In the center was an open space where they cooked their meals, socialized and played cards.

For several years, beginning in the late '80s, Allan and I supported a school that the inmates had established for the children, offering classes in math, English and Nepali. The nicest room in the jail was reserved for the school. We provided furniture, books and other supplies. The prisoners served as the teachers, and there was even a headmaster.

The first time we met the boys, we expected to encounter a bunch of damaged, street-wise, tough little ruffians. Instead, when the prison gate opened, out trotted nine cheerful, playful, curious kids. We dropped by the jail often, bringing sports equipment, clothing, shoes and other treats.

Allan and I would go to the visiting area, a smallish, bare piece of ground outside the prison gate and ask one of the guards standing there with a long rifle to call Arjun, our prison contact who was a trusted inmate and allowed outside the gate. A big, muscular man with a wide smile, he had been a boxer before he got in trouble with the law. Arjun would order the guards to gather up the children and bring them outside to meet us.

After a few months, Arjun asked if we could provide scholarships to some of the boys living in the jail. We agreed and asked him to identify candidates whose fathers were serving long sentences. Without our help, these boys would spend their childhoods in jail, and when they turned 13, they would be evicted to make their way in the world alone.

Whenever Arjun recommended a child to us, Allan and I visited him several times at the jail and then met with his father. If the father gave permission for us to assume custody (no father ever refused), we asked the warden for approval of the arrangement and we signed a statement accepting responsibility for the child's welfare. Some of the boys moved into J House, and we sent others to boarding school. We had an excellent relationship with the jail authorities and brought the children to visit their fathers regularly. Everyone at the jail was pleased to see that the boys were well dressed, healthy, happy and getting a good education.

Early on, Arjun suggested that we give a scholarship to Manish, the youngest boy at the jail. When we arrived to pick him up, we met an adorable little boy, wild with excitement at the prospect of leaving the jail and going to school. Although visitors were not ordinarily allowed inside, the warden gave us permission to see where Manish lived. He showed us the cot he shared with his father and pointed under the bed to show us where he kept his simple belongings. Some small toys were stacked on one corner of the bed. Manish told us this corner was where he played, and indicated another corner where he did his homework. We assured Manish and his father that he would come back to visit regularly, and off we went to J House in our battered, old rented van. This was Manish's first journey in a car, and though he was a bit frightened, he was mesmerized as he rode through the mean streets of Kathmandu on the way to his new home.

Life is brutal for disabled children in Nepal. The social stigma against those with disabilities is pervasive and devastating. J and K Houses sheltered a number of disabled kids—one a paraplegic, others with various other impairments, including blindness or deafness. No one had ever told these children they were important, valued and could contribute to society rather than being viewed as a burden. We were determined to raise them in an inclusive, caring environment where they could learn to love themselves and rise to their full potential.

Bibek was one of the original J House boys. He came to us from Dr. Banskota's hospital after his right arm was amputated above the elbow, following an accident. Bibek grew up in a small village 200 miles from Kathmandu, where he lived with his parents and siblings. His father, an alcoholic, often physically abused his mother. One day, when Bibek could no longer stand by watching as his mother was beaten, he intervened to protect her. In the process, he accidentally struck his father—an unforgivable offense in Nepali society. Realizing that his only alternative was to run away from home, Bibek fled immediately with only the clothes on his back and not a single rupee. He was eight years old.

He ran to the nearest highway and convinced a bus driver to take him, free of charge, to the end of the route. The driver let him off at a roadside settlement several hours from Kathmandu, his destination. To earn money for bus fare to the city, Bibek persuaded the owner of a small eatery along the road to hire him as a dishwasher. The restaurant did not have running water, so several times a day Bibek fetched water from a tap across the road and carried it back in a bucket. One day, when he had saved almost enough money for the bus fare to Kathmandu, a truck hit him as he was running to the tap.

Seriously injured, Bibek was rushed to Bir Hospital, the government hospital in Kathmandu, where his right arm was amputated above the elbow. Later, he was transferred to Dr. Banskota's hospital. In great pain, both physically and psychologically, he spent almost a year recuperating there. Bibek had no idea where he would go or what he would do after he was discharged.

A social worker at the hospital approached me to ask if our foundation could "please, please give Bibek a scholarship." When I went to meet him, a little boy with crisp black hair and a wide, joyful smile bounded into the room where I was waiting. It was difficult to grasp that this was the same kid the social worker had described as having suffered such severe trauma. The stump of his right arm was bandaged, but he threw his left arm around me and hugged me tightly. I was captivated.

Bibek moved into J House in 1992, shortly after it was established. He was the most friendly, affectionate little boy and immediately connected with the other kids. His confident, can-do approach to life was astonishing. He attended an excellent private school, and was a popular student. His passion was basketball. When he first told me that he was going to try out for the basketball team, I blanched. I knew he felt invincible and as capable as any of his classmates in spite of his missing right arm, but who ever heard of a one-armed basketball player? I need not have worried. He made the team and played successfully for the school in many tournaments.

Pashupatinath, a temple complex in Kathmandu, is the holiest religious site in the country. It is the kingdom of beggarhood in Nepal, where the poor and maimed congregate to practice the ancient art of panhandling. Sajani Amatya, a young social worker I had met at Paropakar several years before, told us about a number of little girls who spent their days begging for rupees at the temple, sometimes alone, sometimes accompanied by a parent. Unless these children found a permanent home, they would be prime targets for sexual abuse and, in a few years, for trafficking to the brothels of Bombay. Sajani offered to visit their parents or guardians and ask permission for them to come to live at the newly established K House. In a few days, she returned with good news: one mother, one father, one grandfather and a guardian had all agreed.

The next morning, Allan and I went to Pashupatinath to meet the families of the girls and bring them to K House. Our van was surrounded by small beggar children thrusting their little tin bowls in our faces, repeating a plea for rupees in a monotone like a mantra. I doubt if there was a single child who would not have gladly come with us that morning. There, among the half-naked *sadhus* (holy men) performing their morning ablutions in the public fountain, pilgrims in tattered clothes, gawking tourists and mourning families about to cremate their loved ones, were four adorable, cheerful little girls, impatient to see their new home.

We piled them into our van and drove them to K House. Into the shower they went for shampoos with special anti-lice soap, a thorough scrubbing, and a rubdown with clean towels. Their clothes, crawling with vermin, were discarded immediately and they were given beautiful, new donated outfits.

Five-year-old Maya was one of those girls. She and her grizzled, old father lived in a cramped concrete room on the grounds of the temple complex. The room was totally dark with no electricity, windows or furniture. A few shreds of clothing were tossed over a rope that stretched across the room.

Each morning, as Maya sleepily emerged from under the quilt that protected her from the bone-chilling cold, her father lit a fire in a smoky corner of the room and prepared a breakfast of rice and lentils. Maya washed her face from a pot of cold water and donned a little crown of paper flowers that her father had bought with his meager earnings. Before they left, they locked the door behind them, not only to keep out human intruders, but also to deter the monkeys that ran freely throughout the temple complex and into their room. These were not the beguiling little creatures we see frolicking at the zoo, but large, aggressive, ill-tempered and hungry beasts that snatched and scratched without warning.

Maya and her father walked a short distance to their usual spot on the temple grounds, where they spent the day panhandling. A pretty little girl with a radiant smile, she had been begging beside her father as long as she could remember. As she stood shivering in the chill, Maya wondered if the nice lady—Sajani—would come by to talk to her father, as she had for the last three days. When Sajani arrived later that morning, she asked Maya's father to allow his daughter to move into a home for girls, assuring him that she would be well cared for and sent to school. Her father seemed interested. Maya wanted to go with the lady, but only if her father could come too. Sajani explained this would not be possible, but he could visit her every Saturday. The father agreed, and he accompanied Maya and the three other little girls in the van as we set out for K House.

When they arrived, Maya stared in amazement at the big house on the hill. She had never seen anything like it. As soon as they entered, girls dressed in pretty clothes gathered around to welcome her and show her around. They all seemed so happy. They showed Maya the big common room, the kitchen, the bathrooms and the bedrooms where each girl had her own bed. When Maya saw a girl on the swing at the playground, she rushed back outside. She had never seen a swing before. With a push from the girls, she was soon flying through the air. Maya clung to her father as he left, but was comforted when he promised to visit her every Saturday. Her father headed back to his little room, relieved but sorrowful.

Maya loved K House. Her new sisters took to her immediately, showering her with love and attention. She was blessed with a cheerful, sunny disposition and adjusted quickly. Each morning, she walked with the other girls to the school at the bottom of the hill, wearing her new uniform—a dark blue pleated skirt and a light blue blouse.

Only one thing seemed to mar Maya's rollicking nature. She missed her father. Whenever Sajani visited K House, Maya rushed over to her, suddenly looking sad and serious. She asked longingly,

"Does my father weep for me?" Her father visited on a few Saturdays, bringing her fruit and little gifts. But one Saturday he didn't show up. He missed the next two Saturdays as well. Maya was worried. One of the staff members from of our foundation went to Pashupatinath to inquire after him. The news was devastating: her father had committed suicide. When he realized his little girl had found a safe haven and would be cared for and educated until she could stand on her own, he took his life.

I was in the States at the time and did not have the terrible task of breaking the news to her. She was inconsolable for a few weeks, but with the support of her K House sisters and the foundation's staff, she gradually reverted to the sunny little being she had always been.

Kathmandu was awash with young boys living on the streets. Although some had run away from home because they were attracted by the glitter of the big city, most had left their villages due to abuse, abandonment or extreme poverty. Dressed in dirty, ragged clothes, barefoot and hungry, they curled up in doorways to sleep at night, wrapped in burlap bags to shelter them from the cold pavement, often hugging a street dog for warmth. They survived by begging, stealing or recycling used plastic bags they collected from festering garbage bins. Some were addicted to drugs and alcohol. Despite their destitute circumstances, the children were a spirited and often amusing bunch, experts in the art of the hustle. Some actually enjoyed street life—the freedom, and sometimes the fun, outweighed the misery.

Once in a while, they were downright comical. One day, I was walking on Durbar Marg, a main street in Kathmandu, where good hotels and restaurants, rich tourists and street children converge. I was accosted by a begging boy about 10 years old, lanky and tall, with thin legs sticking out from his shorts, and a shaved head. He had the most dramatically painful expression on his face. Silently, he extended his hand to show me a fresh gash on his palm. It was a little bloody, but hardly justified his exaggerated histrionic performance. The whole scene was so comical. He knew his hand didn't really hurt, I knew it, and he knew that I knew it. I burst out laughing. He looked at me a little startled for a moment, and then he did the same, both of us caught up in the hilarity of his mock suffering. I thought the performance was worth something, and handed him a five-rupee note. He gave a whoop of joy, and turned cartwheels down the street. The last I saw of him, he was dancing around the corner on his long, bare legs, scarcely able to contain his joy. Never have I received so much pleasure for 15.5 cents.

Almost from the beginning, Allan and I tried to provide assistance to street children. There were no government programs to help them, and they were constantly hassled by the police. We linked up with Child Workers in Nepal (CWIN), an organization founded by several young, idealistic Nepali graduate students who were passionate advocates for the rights of impoverished children. Their organization had opened a shelter in a crowded, rundown area of Kathmandu, where they conducted rudimentary classes and provided one meal a day for homeless children.

CWIN operated on a shoestring, as the founders took turns working to raise cash to support the program. We helped when we could by buying shoes for the regulars at the shelter and funding a sick room. Because these children were unable to pay for services, hospitals were reluctant to admit them and they were occasionally found dead on the street after a cold night.

The shelter was running out of money to provide a daily meal to the boys who showed up. The government of Nepal prohibited CWIN from applying for funds from the many non-governmental organizations that proliferated in Kathmandu because one of its founders had criticized the royal family in public—a serious offense. "The hell with that," Allan and I said. When I returned to California, I raised money to support the nourishment program for a year. As it turned out, our help was not needed. In the interim, democracy had come to Nepal. In 1990, huge masses of people demonstrated against the monarchy. As a result, the absolute power of the royal family was diminished. CWIN eventually became a well-funded, powerful advocate for the rights of impoverished children, and remains so to this day.

As much as our hearts went out to the homeless boys, we were cautious about bringing them to J House. We knew that children who had lived on the street for a long time were often unable to adjust to the discipline of a structured home and school. The staff at CWIN kept their eyes open, looking for suitable prospects they thought would be able to adapt to life at the house.

One day, we received a call from them about an eight-year-old boy named Prem. We went to meet him at the shelter where he was living and found a shy, vulnerable, tiny boy with gorgeous black eyes and a mischievous smile. He smelled so bad that I found it difficult to sit close to him. Prem told us that he was eager to get off the street and into school, so we bundled him into our van and headed to J House. Like Manish, it was the first time Prem had ever ridden in a car and he was glued to the window for the entire trip.

The first step with a street kid is a bath and a haircut. Two of the formerly homeless boys took Prem down the street to the barber, who wet his hair, divided it into sections and shaved it off. Rivulets of black water ran down his neck as his lice-ridden hair fell to the floor. Then it was back to J House for a bath. The kitchen helpers spent an hour scrubbing every inch of his little body. Afterwards, Prem appeared clean and smiling, dressed in new sweatpants, a red-striped sweater and a wool hat that covered his newly shorn head. It was a remarkable transformation.

The other kids immediately surrounded Prem, eager to get to know him. One of them, a formerly homeless boy who had arrived at J House a few months earlier, gave Prem his most precious possession—a windup motorcycle. He put his arm around Prem, showed him the book he was reading in kindergarten and told him how happy he would be in his new home. This may have been the first night Prem had ever slept in a warm bed with a full stomach.

CHAPTER NINE

FAMILY LIFE

With no experience running a children's home, Allan and I had to learn by trial and error. We were operating on a low budget with very few staff members, and the older boys at J House acted as our good right hand. Over time, we learned what it takes to provide a secure, loving environment where children thrive.

From the time J House opened in 1992, we were bombarded with desperate pleas for help. Young mothers who had been abandoned by their husbands arrived at our door begging us to take their babies. Impoverished college students came seeking scholarship support. Kind-hearted strangers dropped off destitute children they had found on the street. The older boys acted as translators, helping us to assess which needs were genuine and to find appropriate solutions. They made sure that we were not hoodwinked by strangers seeking an easy handout.

We learned a lot from the J House boys; some of them were more experienced with the harsh realities of Nepal than we were. They were street smart, savvy, wise beyond their years and world-class negotiators. We would buy supplies for the children—clothes, shoes and toothbrushes—shopping for bargains at a vast outdoor market in downtown Kathmandu's Ratna Park. When we returned to J House with our purchases and they found out what we paid, some of the boys looked at each other with consternation—and at us with a hint of condescension. Bhim, a boy who had lived on the street for three years, asked if he could come with us the next time we went shopping. When Allan and I arrived at the market, he instructed us to walk around and discreetly point out what we wanted to buy. Then he told us, "Stay out of sight." As we cowered behind a tree, Bhim went into the crowd, bargaining furiously, cajoling, accusing and walking away indignantly. After an hour or so, he returned with a big grin and presented us with the items we wanted, purchased at half the asking price.

From the beginning, we knew that we wanted to give the children at J and K Houses every advantage, so they could become productive, well-adjusted adults. The kids attend excellent private schools suited to their abilities. We make sure they have nice clothes, good food and outstanding medical care. Each house has a library as well as computers and a TV set, and we encourage them to participate in sports. The children especially love soccer and basketball.

J House has a resident "uncle" and "aunty" who act as surrogate parents, while K House is run by a wise and loving "aunty" who oversees the girls. The warm and supportive atmosphere at the houses is contagious. When children move in, no matter how dreadful their backgrounds, they adapt quickly to their new environment. One seven-year-old runaway, who left home to escape the brutal beatings of his father, arrived at J House with his dukes up and his eyes blazing. Within a week, he realized that he had reached a safe place where he no longer had to defend himself, and he became a helpful, affectionate brother to the other boys.

We treat the children gently and respectfully, and do not allow physical abuse at home or at school. They form close, loving bonds with one another and knit themselves into a tight, protective family, helping each other with schoolwork or personal problems without being asked, and often without our knowledge. The older kids instinctively take responsibility for the younger ones, as if caring for one another is the most natural thing in the world. They wash the clothes of their little sisters and brothers, put them to bed at night and teach them everything from dancing to building Lego masterpieces. It's impossible to know who owns what, since they share all their possessions, including games, toys, books and every piece of clothing. To my knowledge, there has never been a physical confrontation among the kids, and I've never heard them quarrel or even say anything nasty about one another. Of course, it's possible that this behavior has occurred, but I've never witnessed it or heard about it. They refer to each other as "brother" and "sister," and they mean it. And they call me "Olga Mommy" or "Olga Mom."

Sometimes, this devotion manifests itself in unexpected ways. One of the street kids, a lanky teenager, the tallest boy at J House, woke up one morning in December and noticed that the weather was getting cold. He decided that Asmita, the tiniest girl at K House, needed a warm hat, so he knitted her a little red beret.

The children are particularly caring with the disabled kids. Several years ago, during a long school holiday, one of the older boys started a jogging program. The weather was freezing cold, so the daily regimen did not last long, but while it did, the kids ran along back roads, bridges and trails behind the house at dawn. Practically everyone went, even little Asmita. The children didn't want Sanjay, who is paraplegic, to feel left out, so they brought him along and took turns running with the wheelchair. If Sanjay's wheelchair could not be accommodated on an outing, they carried him on their backs. Several boys taught themselves sign language to communicate with Prakash, who is deaf, and there was always someone around to lead the blind kids if they could not navigate on their own.

The J and K House kids were unfailingly loving and helpful toward Allan and me. They don't always do what they are told, but outright confrontation or defiance is rare. At times, they are almost too compliant.

Dashain, the most important festival of the year, is a joyous family event observed for 15 days in the fall with countless blessings, feasts and rituals. It is traditional for Nepalis to buy new clothes for the festival, and for the kids, this is one of the highlights of the season. A couple of weeks before the holiday, we take the children to a decidedly down-scale clothing shop where they can choose from a variety of pants, shirts, shoes, sweaters, hats, belts and dresses. The clothing is of pretty poor quality, but you wouldn't know it from the excitement this shopping spree generates.

As I hunker down in a chair in the shop, the fashion show begins. The kids run around the store, choosing a pair of pants here, a dress there, and then rush over to show me, draping the clothes over their bodies, modeling them for my approval. If, as sometimes happens, I don't like an item, they return it, select something else and come running back to show off another outfit. There is never a hint of resentment or disappointment.

This lack of defiance might be worrisome in a western context, but Nepal has a culture of respect for older people. Even in nuclear families, it is rare for children to sass their parents. Except for a period in the late '90s, when some of the teenage boys began acting out at home and in school, we have not had to confront many behavioral issues. In a handful of cases, we transferred disruptive boys to a boarding school, where their behavior improved under more stringent rules than the easy-going environment at J House.

One of the most intransigent of these kids was Ratna, a boy who came to us at the age of seven from the usual horrific background. He was one of the smartest boys at J House and got along well with the other kids, but he misbehaved at school and was expelled several times. We transferred him to a boarding high school which had a more disciplined environment than J House, and he finally graduated. In college, however, the problems resurfaced. Though Ratna was not violent, he was disruptive. One college reported back to us that he smoked marijuana. When he showed up at the foundation office with all his possessions in a big, black duffel bag after being expelled from college for the second time, we realized that he needed a break from school—something to do and a place to live.

In desperation, we came up with a somewhat unconventional solution. A school we were affiliated with had leased a farm just outside Kathmandu. There was a stable with four riding horses that were being cared for by a professional who needed an assistant, and a rather primitive room on the property where Ratna could live. Somewhat reluctantly, he agreed to the arrangement. He had no alternative. To our surprise, he proved to have a natural affinity for horses. He learned to handle them properly and they responded well to his care. I began to think of him as a "horse whisperer." Perhaps for the first time in his life, he felt real affection and responsibility for another living creature. Ratna's confidence, self-control and self-esteem grew over the following two years, until we were convinced that he was ready to complete his education. We enrolled him in college to train as a veterinarian; he has graduated, and is practicing as a vet in southern Nepal.

The caste system is among the most vicious, divisive and oppressive social systems in the world. The lowest "untouchable" caste members are considered to be impure and polluted. J and K House kids come from many castes, from the highest to the lowest, and they interact with each other with no thought about their differences. Although we don't lecture the children about the need to treat each other fairly, regardless of their caste, religion or ethnic group, they learn from living together that these differences don't matter. Manish, the five year-old boy we brought to J House from the jail, was the only Muslim at the House. When someone cautioned us about bringing a boy so different to live there, I replied, "Just watch our kids." Not surprisingly, the boys embraced him when he arrived, literally and figuratively, and made him feel welcome, loved and secure. This may not seem like a big deal, but in Nepal's caste-conscious culture these differences are taken seriously, particularly in rural areas.

A number of years ago, we interviewed a woman for a job as an assistant cook. A distinctive feature of the caste system is that persons of low caste may not touch or prepare food for those of a higher caste for fear of pollution. One of our employees remarked that the job seeker belonged to the "untouchable" caste, while some of the boys at J House were Brahmin, the highest caste. "Good," we said and hired her on the spot. She was qualified for the job and we wanted to send the message to our kids that all human beings are equally worthy and deserve an equal chance. As expected, the boys treated her with the same courtesy and respect as all the other J House staff members.

Despite their wretched backgrounds, the younger children show few signs of worry, depression, anger or antisocial behavior. They don't complain or dwell on their misfortunes. But beneath their cheerful demeanor, some of them carry deep scars from their past. This manifested itself at the 65th birthday party for Tot Heffelfinger, the surrogate father to Anjita in San Francisco. Tot and Joanne visited Nepal a number of times and were devoted to the children at J and K Houses. The party was a festive affair even though, as often happens in Kathmandu, there was no electricity. The living room was decorated with crepe paper streamers and colorful drawings and there were funny masks for the kids and a silly hat for Tot. The children provided the entertainment: dancing, telling jokes and playing music on the drum and the flute.

At one point in the evening, Robin, a formerly homeless boy, now a teenager, picked up the guitar and began to sing a song he had composed. The room suddenly fell silent. Sitting in his wheelchair, Sanjay, who had been cutting up a few seconds before, looked as though he was about to cry. Ankit, whose little spaghetti body had been undulating from head to toe around the dance floor, looked utterly dejected. In fact, all the kids seemed inexpressibly sad. This somber mood lasted only a short time, until the room exploded into hijinks once again, but it was a telling moment. Later, when we asked for a translation of the lyrics, we understood the sudden change of mood. Robin sang about an idyllic life in his village, when he had a mother and father and life was sweet. The chorus, repeated after each stanza, described life as an uphill struggle, filled with the pain of loss and separation. Although cheerful on the surface, Robin had composed a number of songs and poems imbued with an underlying theme of deep sadness.

As kids in the houses grow older, they begin to feel more acutely the absence of a nuclear family. Because family is everything in Nepal, we do our best to help them stay in touch with a parent or relative. Our foundation frequently pays the traveling expenses for families to visit their children. Some of them have no recollection of how they got to us, and don't know the whereabouts of their relatives, but we usually have some information about the village they came from and we try our best to contact any family they may have there. If a child wishes, we encourage a visit to their families if it is safe to do so. For those who are too young to travel alone, an older "brother" or "sister" from the houses accompanies them, or a relative may come from the village to fetch them. Most of the time, their relatives remember them and welcome them warmly, and they are able to rebuild family bonds. Sometimes, however, the visits are not successful and the child returns feeling sad and rejected.

To meet these challenges, in 2006 the Nepal Youth Foundation established the Ankur Psychosocial Counseling Center, the only counseling center in the country devoted to children. J and K House children receive regular counseling on an individual basis and in groups, and all the children in our programs can avail themselves of its services. The center continues to offer help to our kids through college and beyond.

Problems experienced by kids in the West, such as experimenting with drugs and alcohol or violent behavior, are not common in Nepal. Gun violence is not an issue because weapons are strictly prohibited by law—only the Army, some police and a limited number of citizens are allowed to possess them. As for problems related to underage sex, there has never been a single case of pregnancy out of wedlock in the 20 years since we opened K House.

The mood at the houses is cheerful, upbeat and animated. After the kids finish their homework in the afternoon, they gather in the living room to play hand-clapping games, tell jokes, tease each other, do jigsaw puzzles and fool around with the little ones. They love to dance, and no stranger is allowed to sit by just watching. No matter how old or infirm visitors may be, the kids take their hands, haul them to their feet and encourage them to wriggle and writhe until the room is bursting with loud music and shimmying bodies. They howl with laughter when I show them a few moves from my jitterbugging days.

We celebrate traditional Nepali holidays as well as Christmas, although it is not observed in most of the country. Father Christmas— our driver or another paunchy guy— arrives attired in a big red suit with a bushy white beard, carrying a basket filled with colorful stockings stuffed with gifts. Western kids would find the contents unexciting, to say the least—a scarf, a couple of pieces of candy, a small plastic toy, a wool hat, an orange. But our kids pore over these simple treasures with delight and appreciation.

During school holidays or weekends, we take the kids on outings— swimming, biking or hiking. They enjoy these activities, but what they look forward to most is our annual three-day adventure during their winter vacation when we go to a mountain village, a resort town on a lake or a national park. For some of them, this is the first time they've witnessed the stunning natural beauty of their country and realize that there is more to Nepal than the crowded, dirty, polluted streets of Kathmandu. These excursions also open their eyes to the difficulties of life in rural Nepal. They see children their own age carrying heavy loads of fodder on their backs or working in the fields, many with no opportunity to go to school. Our kids return home from these outings with a renewed appreciation for the opportunities they've been given.

Their favorite destination is one of the wildlife parks on the southern border with India. On one particularly memorable excursion, a baby rhino came ambling up to the lodge where we were staying. The villagers adopted this darling, fat little creature after his mother was killed by a poacher. Although they tried to return him to the wild, he kept coming back and eventually he became a sort of a village mascot. The locals never even bothered to look up as the baby rhino ambled along the dirt road past shops and houses. Our kids, however, were thrilled when he wandered close enough to munch grass and leaves from their hands.

The kids loved riding on the back of an elephant, six or eight at a time, hoping to get a glimpse of rhinos sunning themselves in the tall grass. But what they liked best of all was helping to bathe the elephants in the river. As the behemoths submerged themselves in the muddy water for their baths at the end of the day, the children helped the *mahout* (elephant driver) scrub the dust from the elephant's hide with stones. When the job was finished, three or four kids climbed on the back of the elephant and, as the great hulk slowly rose out of the water, they were tossed off into the river, screaming with pleasure.

In the evening, the villagers, dressed in their local costumes, performed the traditional dances of their ethnic community, singing and swirling around a huge bonfire to the rhythmic beat of homemade drums. On one of these trips, as the dancers darted around the flames, I noticed one of the teenage boys cradling three-year-old Alok in his arms, the newest and youngest boy at J House, crooning to him softly as he rocked him to sleep. "We must be doing something right," I thought to myself as I slipped off to bed.

Back in Kathmandu, each year I invite the K House girls, 10 at a time, to a sleepover at my house during their winter school holiday. After their favorite dinner of *momos* (dumplings) and chicken, they hop into a bubble bath, three at a time. Like most Nepalis, the girls new to K House have never been immersed in hot water and are initially scared to even dip a toe in. But once they plop down into the tub, it's difficult to get them out. They squeal with laughter and splash each other until there's almost as much water on the bathroom floor as in the tub. The older girls see to it that their little sisters are actually soaped down and shampooed. After their bath, they run downstairs wrapped in towels to dry off in front of a roaring fire in the living room before donning their pajamas. When the little girls are tucked into bed—usually four to a bed, though they assure me more can fit—the teenagers and I sit around the fire and talk about life. During these chats, I occasionally say, "Now, girls, give me the lowdown. I never hear you argue or even say anything bad about one another. Don't you ever fight or squabble?" They admit that they disagree occasionally, yet they always add, "but we really love each other!"

One evening at a sleepover, I casually asked the girls if they had ever seen an iPad. They almost swooned when I showed them mine. iPads were rare in Nepal at the time—and very expensive. None of them had actually seen one, though they had heard of them. Like teenagers everywhere, it wasn't long before they learned how to navigate all the icons—something that took me hours to master. They stayed up for several hours after I went to bed, taking turns pounding away on the screen. A couple of days later, almost by accident, I tapped the "Notes" icon on my iPad and found a bunch of messages from them. Here are some of their notes, complete with teenage slang and punctuation:

> *Today is the first day of me . . . using an iPad and it is so wonderful!! IT WAS ALWAYS MY DREAM!! . . .When I finish my study, I want to be person like you and I will do my best in my future and definitely I will buy an iPad. Thank you Mom for everything you have done for us. We will always remember you. Because of you we are able to use iPad . . . omg . . . iPad!!!!!!!!!!!*
>
> *After dinner we had lots of talks with Olga Mom . . .We learned many things with her!! We should learn to stay happy . . . We should learn to be thankful for everything that we've got!! Sometimes it doesn't work as we want and that totally makes us down . . . but we have to learn to cope with it!! Our life is not always fun and interesting. It is filled with problems!! But without problems our life won't be interesting at all . . . We get problems . . . why? . . . to cope with it! . . . to learn many new things in life! To know that our life is not always easy!! I am happy to live my life like this!! I am so happy for all the things I have got.*
>
> *I'm not able to write more because I ate too much and my stomach is going to blast so I'm stopping to write but I will write you an email when I buy an iPad . . . ok Mom.????*
>
> *Our Beautiful Mom ROCKS!"*

Realizing that they would not be able to buy an iPad any time soon, the next day the girls went home and made iPads for themselves out of cardboard, complete with sequins, hearts, stickers, ribbons and even an icon called "girls games."

What I find most poignant about these positive, spirited and confident messages is the backdrop of the girls' lives. One had been bonded away by her alcoholic father as a servant when she was seven years old. Another followed her sight-impaired mother around as she begged on the filthy streets of Kathmandu. A third lost both parents to snakebites when she was six years old.

The children are aware of their good fortune and show it in many ways. It is not customary to say grace before meals in Hindu culture, but a number of years ago, the girls asked their K House "uncle" to compose a prayer to express their thanks for their new lives. For several months, they started dinner with these words: "Oh God, let us have the privilege to give you our innermost thanks for providing us proper education, food, clothing and shelter. We also pray that these things be granted to children who live in different parts of the world in destitution. Help us to be authentic human beings in the world." The girls recited this little prayer with the utmost intensity, hands clasped, eyes shut tight, with a different girl leading the recitation each night.

They express their gratitude through action as well. On Environmental Awareness Day, the children pitch in to clean the filthy Bagmati River in Kathmandu. They have contributed from their small allowances to help young flood victims in Western Nepal, as well as children living with HIV/AIDS. Sometimes, they produce original artwork, greeting cards and handicrafts, or cook Nepali meals which they sell at outrageous prices to raise money for various causes serving disadvantaged children. Occasionally, we take them camping near an isolated village where they bandage wounds, teach English to the local school children and give lessons in tooth brushing, guitar playing and dancing. When a J or K House child is hospitalized, one of the older kids stays with him or her day and night, sleeping on the floor by the bedside, tutoring the patient to keep up with schoolwork and providing care, comfort and nutritious food brought from home.

Years ago, when we were visiting Kanti Children's Hospital regularly to assist needy children, we sent one of the older J House boys to the hospital during his winter vacation to identify patients who needed our help. Bimal was perfect for the job. Somewhat impaired himself, he had an uncanny empathy for the sick and disabled. He had appointed himself the prime caretaker for Sanjay, the paraplegic boy at J House, and looked after him like a tender, loving mother. He was so selfless and thoughtful that I used to call him a teenage, male Mother Teresa.

One day, Bimal returned to J House from the hospital, eyes shining, brimming with happiness. He told us that he had saved the lives of two very poor, severely ill children that day. They had been admitted to Kanti and needed blood transfusions immediately. At that time, blood was not available for purchase in Nepal, but the Red Cross would provide it if they had it on hand. The catch was that the parents did not have the $3 required for the plastic bag and tubing needed to administer the transfusion. Bimal called the Red Cross and found that the right type of blood was available. He took a taxi to pick up the blood, paid for the needed accessories and rushed back to the hospital. The two children received transfusions and, happily, they survived.

Long after the J and K House children grow up, many of them come back to visit me, to talk about their lives and introduce me to their spouses and children. As I sit in my beautiful garden in Kathmandu chatting away with these self-confident young adults, I think back to the time they first came into my life, and I am filled with gratitude and awe at what they have become.

Recently, Sheela came to visit with her husband and baby. She is a college graduate and teaches at a private school. As I looked at the happy, healthy, confident young woman before me, I thought back with wonder to the tiny beggar girl who came to K House from a temple complex 20 years ago. Sheela was frightened, filthy, hungry, with no prospects for an education. If we had not rescued her, there is a good chance she would have been trafficked years ago.

One of the four boys from Paropakar Orphanage who received a college scholarship in 1985 has spent his entire career teaching at a school for handicapped children. He had problems passing the college entrance exams, but we stuck with him, providing him with extra tutoring until he did so. Now in his 40s, he visits me regularly with his two sons, who are about the same age he was when I met him. They are both brilliant students about to graduate from engineering school.

Alisha, the wild-looking six-year-old girl who lived in a tiny village high in the Himalayas, where the local school only went to 3rd grade, proved to be a first rate student. After high school, she received a full scholarship to Colby-Sawyer College in New Hampshire, graduating with a bachelor's degree in environmental science. She plans to get a Masters degree and then return to Nepal to work on environmental issues.

And then there is Kumar, a little boy we removed from jail, where he was living with his father. He attended a good private boarding school, graduated, and went on to college. He wrote to Som in his senior year, "It feels like yesterday when I was living a miserable life in prison, and then how happy I was when studying in Gyanodya. I look behind and compared my life. I might have been in my village joined in some gang and playing battle, scaring people, looting and creating violence to the society, but today I am someone because of you all…I promise that I will do something for my community and helpless people because that is what you have taught me."

Kumar has been true to his word. Following graduation from college, he created a program in his home village to build an ecologically sustainable, agro-tourist enterprise that will bring income to the village, train farmers in environmentally sound practices and retain young people in the community by providing them with a way to earn a living. He is married to a delightful young woman and they have a new baby. And now he is back with the Nepal Youth Foundation—this time working as Som's right-hand man.

And what has become of the four children who joined the J and K House family shortly after the houses were established? Prem, the street boy, joined the Maoist insurgency, but became disillusioned with the rebels and left their army. He works in the Gulf States now, and continues his avid interest in Nepali politics. Manish, the 5 year-old we rescued from jail, has grown into a tall, handsome young man about to graduate from college with a degree in business. Maya, the little beggar girl at Pashupatinath, has evolved into a beautiful, stylish, warm and charming young woman. She graduated from St. Xavier's College, one of the best colleges in Nepal, with a bachelor's degree in social work. She has a job with a domestic airline, but she hopes to follow her dream of becoming a social worker in the future. Maya still has the little paper crown of flowers she was wearing the day she moved to K House 20 years ago.

Bibek, who came to us from the Jorpati hospital after he lost his right arm, is in his early 30s and lives in the United States. He has an MBA from Dominican University in California, works in the IT sector and is engaged to a young woman who is as happy, solid and fun-loving as he is. He hasn't lost his explosive optimism, his "can do" spirit, or the radiant, dazzling smile that blew me away so long ago. Bibek appeared with me on The Oprah Winfrey Show in 2002 and made a statement to the world that says it all. When Oprah asked him about the loss of his arm, he replied, "Losing my arm has been more of a blessing than a curse. If that had not happened, I would be homeless on the street. I would be nobody."

Anjita and me shortly after her arrival in the U.S.

At Kathmandu airport with Anjita and Paru, about to depart for the U.S.

Anjita at age fourteen

Joanne and Tot Heffelfinger with Anjita

Shanta, a blind girl, and some of her medals for athletic performance

Little boys at the jail before their rescue

Manish on his way from jail to J House

Maya at K House

Maya and her father at Pashupatinath temple complex

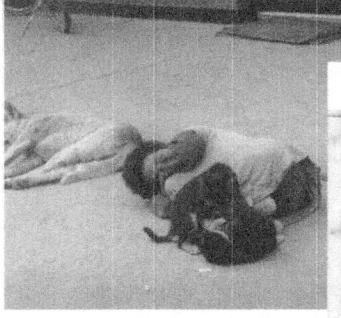

Homeless boy sleeping on street with dog for warmth

First J House boys

Riding an elephant
at a wildlife park

Four girls to a bed at a
sleepover party at my house

K House girls with puppy

Girlie iPad made by K House girls
with hearts, ribbons and game icons

Art class

Father Christmas brings gifts for the children at J and K House

Little J House Boys

Young woman raised at K House returns for a visit

Time for homework

K House girls love
hand-clapping games

J House boys fooling around

Som with the second generation
of J House boys

Second generation of K House girls

CHAPTER TEN

CHANGES AND CHALLENGES

When I first offered college scholarships to four boys from Paropakar Orphanage in 1985, I never dreamed that within a decade Allan and I would be running a nonprofit foundation, supporting several hundred scholarship students and raising 60 kids at J and K Houses. We had come a long way from the "files-in-tin-trunks-under-the-bed" stage, and the Nepal Youth Foundation finally had a real office. We set up shop in one room of a flat that was occupied by several former J House boys who were attending college in Kathmandu. Not only that—we hired our first employee to help us administer the program.

By 1994, Allan and I realized that we needed extra help. Because we were both spending only part of each year in Nepal, we wanted to find someone who could stay closely connected with the scholarship students as well as the kids and staff at J and K Houses during our absence. In addition, since our foundation was officially registered with the government of Nepal as an international non-governmental organization, we needed a local employee who could deal with the frustrating bureaucratic hoops we often had to jump through.

We agreed that we needed to hire a Nepali and almost simultaneously came up with the same candidate for the job. "How about Som Paneru?" Som was one of the most gifted students that NYF had supported through college. In December of 1994, we invited him to dinner at the Old Vienna Inn, a casual tourist restaurant in Kathmandu that was always packed with boisterous young trekkers. Over dinner, we offered him the handsome sum of $70 a month to work for the foundation.

"When I walked into the restaurant," Som recalls, "it seemed quite foreign to me. It was the fanciest place I had ever seen. I was impressed by the pictures on the walls, the napkins, cutlery and glassware. I had no idea why Olga and Allan had invited me to dinner, but when they offered me a job, I accepted eagerly."

Som was born in September 1967 in the Gorkha District of Nepal, a mountainous region located 100 miles northwest of Kathmandu. His family lived in a remote village that was a two-day walk from the nearest paved road. The villagers eked out a living by subsistence farming, raising mostly corn, millet, rice and vegetables.

Like all the villagers, Som looked forward to the Dashain festival celebrated by Nepalis in the fall of each year. "This was the only time of the year when we could get a really good meal and buy new clothes," he remembers. "We celebrated by feasting on goat meat curry and beaten rice. Except for Dashain, we were lucky if we had goat meat once or twice a year, though we knew we would always have it when our mother gave birth to a child."

Som's father, a religious Brahmin, was a strict disciplinarian who ruled over his nine children with an iron fist. Every day before and after school, the children worked in the fields, herded cattle and collected fodder until dark. "One of my chores was to take the cattle across the shallow river and into the nearby forest for grazing," he recalls. "When we reached the river, we often made a little bamboo trap to catch fish and crabs. Then we would light a fire, cook the fish and eat them while sitting on the banks of the river. If we spotted a leopard or a jackal when we got to the forest, we would yell and throw stones to chase the animal away."

Rising at dawn, the children did chores until it was time to walk the three miles to school, scrambling up and down steep mountain trails for over an hour. "We were always in a hurry to get to school on time after finishing our chores," Som says. "One section of the trail was so scary that my siblings and I held hands to keep from tumbling over a treacherous cliff.

"Coming home after school was a different story. We looked forward to the afternoon walk home as our bonus time. On days when we got out of school early, we had several hours of free time before our father expected us home to work. We played games, ran around and climbed trees to steal bananas. After supper, when our chores were done, we studied by the light of a smoky kerosene lamp, as there was no electricity in our village."

When Som was in 7th grade, Preb Stritter, a Peace Corps volunteer, was assigned to teach at his school. Preb was no starry-eyed, newly-minted college graduate. She was a woman in her 60s with four grown children, who had spent her working life as a math teacher in New

England schools. After their children left home, Preb and her husband moved to rural Vermont, where they lived in a small cabin heated by a wood stove. When her husband died, Preb joined the Peace Corps and was sent to Nepal. She lived in a little dirt-floored house on the school grounds near Som's village.

"Sometimes when we walked by Preb's hut," Som recalls, "we could smell something delicious baking in her clay fire pit. We were always pleased when she invited us to stop for biscuits or homemade cookies."

She controlled her classes with a firm hand. Som was awed by this no-nonsense woman who was so unlike anyone he had ever met before. He admired her immense knowledge and her fierce determination to educate her students. "Preb had a very different way of teaching math," says Som. "She wanted us to understand the reasoning behind the principles of geometry, not just memorize the basics, as Nepali teachers did. Though we were all a little afraid of her and thought she was too strict, Preb was a very good teacher. And unlike Nepali teachers, she never hit us with a stick to punish us."

When he was 13 years old, Som ran away from home. He dreamed of getting a better education than the village school could provide and repeatedly implored his father to send him to boarding school. But the family could not afford a private school education. One night, when his father was sleeping, Som stole 360 rupees from his pocket—a few dollars. At dawn the next morning, he quietly jumped off the deck of the house so as not to wake his sleeping family and headed for Kathmandu to the home of an uncle he hoped would fulfill his wish of going to private school.

Som knew the way to the bus station in the village of Khaireni. Ever since he was a young boy, he had accompanied his father to buy salt and spices, the only commodities the family needed to purchase. Many times, they had crossed the dangerous Daraundi River, walked two days over rough trails to reach the town, and returned home carrying the salt and spices on their backs. On his runaway adventure, Som walked to Khaireni, where he boarded a bus bound for Kathmandu. He found his way to his uncle's house and proudly announced that he was going to enroll himself in boarding school. "And who is going to pay to send you to a private school?" asked his uncle. He confiscated the remaining rupees and sent Som back to his village.

After Som graduated from 8th grade, he received a scholarship to the Gandaki Boarding School in Pokhara, a private school run by the United Missions to Nepal, a consortium of Protestant charities. The organization awarded scholarships annually to two gifted students from each of Nepal's 75 districts, and Som was chosen from Gorkha. "Going to school at Gandaki fulfilled a fantasy I had since 5th grade to attend an excellent school," Som says. "I felt as if I was suffocating in my village. Gandaki had a beautiful campus with many acres of land. We ate in a big dining hall and had fantastic food so different from the limited diet I had eaten all my life, and we played sports every day—soccer, basketball and cricket. My favorite was running. Every Friday night, we watched movies or had other entertainment. I had my photograph taken for the first time and I still have that student identification card."

At Gandaki, Som was exposed to an exciting new world of knowledge and opportunities that he could not have imagined as a Gorkha schoolboy. "We had very good teachers. They were kind to us and never used a stick for punishment. Even though there were 300 boys in the school, I felt like I was part of a very large family. When I look back, I think of my time there as the three golden years of my life." Som graduated from 10th grade, the end of high school in Nepal, as one of the top three students in his class.

Preb returned to Vermont but kept in touch with Som. An inveterate schoolteacher, she returned Som's letters with corrections and comments in red ink. In these exchanges, Preb repeatedly stressed the importance of an education for a full and happy life.

Som desperately wanted to go to college, but higher education was beyond his family's means and he did not feel it was appropriate to ask Preb for help. He accepted a job as a science teacher at a private school in Kathmandu and tutored students in science and math for the college entrance exams in the mornings and evenings to supplement his meager salary.

Preb was so successful in convincing Som of the importance of education that he not only became a teacher, but he also took responsibility for educating his five younger brothers and sisters. It was a tremendously heroic undertaking for a young man just out of high school.

Som brought his siblings from the village to live with him so they could attend school in Kathmandu. He fed and clothed them, paid their school expenses and tutored them so they would do well in their studies. They lived in one room, with a small kitchen tucked into a corner, and studied at the kitchen table in the evenings. The two girls shared the only bed, while the boys slept on quilts they spread across the floor at night and rolled up in the morning. Occasionally, Som's parents gave them a little cash or supplied rice and vegetables from their farm. Ultimately, Som's five siblings graduated from college and all but one went on to professional careers as journalist, teacher, dentist and engineer.

Preb visited Nepal in 1990 and learned about Som's dream of going to college. I had met Preb in Nepal in 1985 through a mutual friend and had mentioned to her that we were giving scholarships to college students. She offered Som a scholarship to Tribhuvan University, the government college in Kathmandu, and routed the funds through our foundation. Those were the days before we had an office, so sponsored students picked up their grants directly from Allan at Paropakar Orphanage.

"The first time I went to collect my stipend at Paropakar," Som remembers, "I was very surprised to see a foreigner—an old lady with white hair—joking, teasing and playing with the young boys. I was introduced to Olga Murray. The only American woman I had ever met before was Preb—a serious, intimidating New Englander. There was a strict hierarchy among students and teachers in Nepal and it was inappropriate for them to engage in friendly exchanges. Olga's genuine friendliness and kindness toward the boys broke down the traditional barriers between children and adults."

Som's monthly stipend of $40 covered all his college expenses, including room and board, tuition and books. "It was the largest amount of money I had ever held in my hand," says Som. "I stuffed all the cash into my pocket so that no one would steal it and constantly patted my shirt when I walked around to make sure the money was still there. Each month, I bought books and supplies as soon as possible, so I didn't have to worry about carrying all that cash."

He graduated from Tribhuvan University with high honors and a degree in mathematics, physics and chemistry, and decided to continue his teaching career. Science teachers were in great demand all over Nepal, but he chose to work with children in a rural area rather than a private school in Kathmandu. Though his siblings still needed his financial support, they were old enough to manage the household and continue their education without his presence. He accepted a job at a school in Salleri, a village in the Mount Everest area, and was the only college-trained science teacher in the district.

After a year at Salleri, Som was offered a position as assistant to the head of the Social Welfare Council in Kathmandu, the Nepal government agency that deals with international organizations like ours. One of his relatives had been appointed to head the council and, knowing that Som was capable and scrupulously honest, he asked him to move to Kathmandu to work as his aide. A few months later, Som's relative was replaced for political reasons. Som saw the handwriting on the wall and knew that he would be out of a job soon, so he made plans to resume his teaching career.

At this point, Allan and I invited him to dinner at the Old Vienna Inn. Som recalls, "I felt a strong obligation to give back to society some of the benefits I had enjoyed. Many friends from my village who were smart and wanted an education were toiling away in the fields because their families couldn't afford to send them to school. My own education and achievements were in large part due to the encouragement, guidance and assistance of others, mostly Americans. If foreigners were willing to sacrifice the comforts of western life to help Nepali children, I felt that I, as a Nepali, had a duty to help. I had dreamt for years of starting an organization to educate disadvantaged children and went so far as to enlist a colleague at the Social Welfare Council to draft a model charter for a non-governmental organization that I hoped to create some day. So the offer of a job at the foundation was a perfect fit for my aspirations."

After he came to work for us, Som learned about the our work by cruising around Kathmandu with Allan in a beat-up leased white van that they sometimes had to push to get started. They spent time with the children at J and K Houses, met with the scholarship students, visited the schools they attended, consulted with their teachers and worked together at the foundation's office. By this time, we were providing scholarships to students living outside Kathmandu. Part of Som's job was to visit the students and the schools in rural areas to distribute scholarship money and assure that the funds were being utilized properly. He was a quick learner—very smart, creative, good with the children and organized in a way that Allan and I were not.

When Som came to work for NYF, he found not only a job he loved, but a wife as well. Sajani, the young social worker who found Maya and three other little girls begging at the Pashupatinath temple complex, had been a devoted volunteer at NYF before Som came on board. She and Som developed a friendship over many years, cemented by their mutual love for and commitment to Nepali children. In 2007, Som and Sajani were married at a boisterous wedding attended by 1,000 guests, most of them children.

Almost five years after Som came on board, in November 1999, Allan and I parted ways because of a major disagreement about the management of J House. In the late spring of that year, Som sent a distressing message to Allan and me while we were in San Francisco. There were problems with some of the older boys at J House. A handful of them had been expelled from school for misbehaving; they were having difficulties with the neighborhood boys and were increasingly hostile to the house supervisor. Allan and I had an unspoken agreement that he would oversee the children's homes and the staff there, but if there were problems relating to the kids, we would try to resolve them together. Prior to Som's message, I had not been aware of any serious behavior issues at J House.

When Allan returned to Nepal, he tried his best to find a solution. He sent a few boys off to boarding school and tried to reason with the troublesome kids who remained at the house. I followed a few months later, hoping that by the time I arrived the problems would be resolved. But the teenage boys continued to misbehave and were uncooperative at home and at school. The house supervisor threatened to quit. J House was not a happy place. I feared that the younger boys would be affected by the conduct of their older brothers, and that J House would no longer be the cheerful, comforting home that had nurtured so many children for seven years.

Whatever was bothering the older boys had been brewing for a long time. It seemed that neither Allan nor I had a clue as to the underlying cause or how to go about correcting the situation. I felt that because we came from a very different cultural background, we lacked a deep understanding of the boys' problems, fears, insecurities and issues with authority. I told Allan that I thought management of the houses should be turned over to a Nepali, who would have more insight and appreciation of the boys' situation and would be in a better position to find a way forward. Som was the obvious choice. He was young, had grown up poor in a Nepali village and had considerable experience working with teenagers as a teacher and social worker. Beyond that, he was wise, compassionate and familiar with the children at the two houses and the foundation's programs. Allan disagreed and resigned from the foundation. I deeply regretted this break in our long collaboration.

My confidence in Som proved to be fully justified. With his help, J House returned to the happy place it was before the crisis, and continues so to this day. We hired a new couple to supervise the house and provided them with the support and training that allowed them to walk the fine line between love and discipline our boys required. In the 15 years since these events occurred, there have been no serious disciplinary problems at J House.

Although the internal problems at J House were resolved, in 2002, a confrontation with the Maoists threatened the physical safety of the children at both J and K Houses. It was common during the insurgency for members of the Maoist party to seek "donations" from businesses, individuals and nonprofits to support their party's revolutionary activities. Our foundation was among those targeted. One day, a man with a handkerchief over his face appeared in our office in Kathmandu and demanded the rupee equivalent of $1,700 for the Maoist cause. One of our senior employees pleaded with the stranger, telling him that our foundation supports some of the most destitute children in Nepal; he explained that the funds we receive from donors may only be used for this purpose. The stranger was unmoved. He replied that he knew where our children's homes were and what our school bus looked like. He said he would return the next day to pick up the cash and we better have it ready.

We were in a difficult situation. The Maoists had destroyed schools and school busses and many children had been killed in these attacks. We simply could not take a chance. When the stranger appeared the following day, one of our employees handed him the amount he demanded. Incredibly, he provided us with a receipt on Maoist party letterhead! This was apparently to ensure that if another Maoist made a demand of us, we could prove that we had already paid. Later, a member of our board and I repaid the funds to the foundation's treasury so that our donors' money was not used to satisfy an extortion.

Aside from this threat and the confrontation with the Maoists described in Chapter Two, neither the Maoists nor the government interfered with our foundation's activities, and we were able to continue our support for Nepali children. This support extended not only to individuals, but to schools as well, particularly for infrastructure. Most of the government schools in rural Nepal were in disrepair, many seriously so. Sometimes, more than 75 students crammed into a single room, where they sat on the dirt floor, with other students peering through the open windows to try to catch what the teacher was saying. Occasionally, there was no building at all. Classes were held outdoors in the searing heat of summer and the numbing cold of winter, as children sat on empty rice bags brought from home and a single teacher ran back and forth from one group to another. In one community, children sat on the ground in a cowshed while the cows were let out to graze. Over the years, our foundation rebuilt schools or added classrooms at nearly 100 government schools in rural areas. Local villagers donated the physical labor and the land, while we paid for building materials and provided expert assistance with engineering, design and supervision.

Some of the most dilapidated schools we came across were in the Nuwakot District, home to an ethnic group called the Danuwar. They are among the poorest and most marginalized communities in Nepal. The overall literacy rate was 25 percent, and only 30 percent of the girls went to school. Most students dropped out before 5th grade and went to work as laborers to help support their families. Many married in their early teens.

A few of the schools in the area were in such decrepit condition that they presented a serious impediment to learning. The Anpchaur Primary School was located in the middle of the village and had no boundary wall. Parents and others entered the classrooms at will, or yelled through the window to order their children home to work. Unemployed men played cards in front of the school's entrance, while dogs wandered freely in and out of classrooms. The back of the school was used as a toilet. Another school in the district, the Bandevi School, was a 25 year old structure made of mud and stone. It was on the verge of collapse. There were not enough classrooms for each of the five grades, so the students in grades three and four studied in the same room, with third graders facing in one direction, and fourth graders in the other. At the communities' request, we rebuilt the Anpchaur and Bandevi schools, and repaired other dilapidated schools in the area.

NYF gave scholarships to students, primarily girls, to attend the Anpchaur and Bandevi schools, as well as other rural schools. Sponsoring the education of a student at a government school is one of the best bargains imaginable. In theory, it costs nothing to attend a government school, but many parents don't have the money for uniforms, books and the small fee that many schools charge. The annual cost to support a child in a rural school is $50-$100, and the foundation has provided thousands of these scholarships over the years.

Helping individuals in desperate circumstances has been always an important part of our work. We have provided medical care for homeless kids, arranged for surgery by visiting plastic surgeons for disfigured street children, bought quilts for elderly people forced to sleep outside under the cold Kathmandu sky, subsidized heart surgeries for dozens of children, and offered emergency aid to many families.

Early on, we discovered that some of the most urgent needs were at the two government hospitals in Kathmandu—Bir Hospital and Kanti Children's Hospital, which is the only general hospital for children in the country. The government hospitals in Nepal are unlike anything that exists in the United States. Patients arrive accompanied by one or more family members, who sleep on quilts brought from home on the floor between the beds, in the corridors or even outdoors on the hospital grounds. In fact, there are often more relatives than patients on the premises. Although medical care and basic meals are free, the families are expected to supply everything else the patient needs, including food to supplement the unappetizing fare served by the hospital.

They must also attend to their own personal needs—feeding themselves, washing their clothes, bathing and performing other tasks of daily living. And they must do these things in an unfamiliar environment. Many have never ventured far from their villages before and they are confused and intimidated by the big city. Most are dreadfully poor. For some, their entire savings have been spent on the journey to the hospital. Their situation is further aggravated if the doctor recommends a test or medication that the hospital does not provide without payment.

We visited the two hospitals regularly, offering help to families who could not afford costly interventions such as scans or expensive antibiotics. In one case, a young woman who had fallen out of a tree and broken both legs languished in the hospital for weeks because her family could not afford the plates and screws needed for an operation. When I asked the doctor if I could pay for these, he scribbled a prescription on his note pad and directed me to the nearest surgical shop. I returned soon after, toting the hardware in a plastic bag. The doctor performed the surgery free of charge, and the patient went home to resume a normal life.

One of our most memorable interventions at Kanti Children's Hospital not only saved the life of a child, but many years later, we helped him find the love of his life.

While we were visiting one of our children at the hospital, we noticed Bijay, a seven-year-old boy, lying spent and sad in his bed. He was obviously very ill—slight of build, pale and thin, but with an enormous belly. The doctors told us that Bijay was suffering from *kala azar*, a nasty tropical disease caused by the bite of a sand flea. His illness was in an advanced stage, and the only medication available locally had proved to be ineffective.

Bijay's parents had sent him and his slightly older sister to find work in Kathmandu, where they were both employed at a carpet factory. When Bijay became ill, the factory owner did not want to take responsibility for a sick child, so he dropped him at the door of the hospital and hurried off. In truth, the doctors were waiting for Bijay to die. He knew it, and he was terrified. Bijay was almost always alone, since his sister worked long hours at the carpet factory and seldom had time to visit. Even now, I can hardly bear the thought of a young child all alone in the hospital waiting to die, with no one to comfort him.

James Heffelfinger, the son of my friends Joanne and Tot, had just graduated from medical school in New York and was working at the University of California Medical Center in San Francisco. In desperation, I wrote to ask if he knew of some medication that might help. He replied that a colleague told him of a recent discovery—a medication used for many years to alleviate another condition had sometimes proved effective in treating *kala azar*. The hospital was willing to provide it without charge, but because the side effects could be very serious if it was not administered properly, we needed to find a doctor in Kathmandu who had some experience with it. Wonder of wonders, I was able to find an American doctor who had dispensed the medication before and was willing to give it a try. James delivered the medicine personally to the hospital in Kathmandu. The therapy worked as intended, and Bijay recovered fully and left the hospital in blooming good health.

Since he had no place to go after discharge, he moved into J House. Bijay grew into a gentle, helpful, thoroughly nice young man. After high school, he was not interested in going to college, so he attended a vocational school, where he was trained as a cook. He is now in his late 20s and has a good job at a private school. In March 2013, I saw him at the school and asked him to give me a call sometime. Little did I know where this casual comment would lead.

Bijay phoned the next day to tell me that he was very, very sad. Someone had introduced him to a girl he liked very much and hoped to marry, but she had called it off because her parents said he was "just a cook."

In Nepal, arranged marriages are customary for the vast majority of couples. They are carefully managed by a close friend or family member, but the J and K House children do not have such intermediaries. A number of people have asked me over the years what we would do to help the children we have raised when it came time for them to find spouses. My response has always been, "Look, they're well-educated, well-brought up, well-dressed, attractive kids. They'll find their own spouses."

And so they had—until now.

I decided to break my rule and try to find Bijay a wife because he was very shy and needed help. My initial effort was a failure. I asked a Nepali friend if she knew of a prospect, and the first thing she wanted to know was what caste he belonged to. The caste issue had never crossed my mind and I was somewhat taken aback. Bijay is a Dalit, an "untouchable," a member of the lowest caste. The young woman my friend had in mind was a Brahmin, the highest caste. She made it clear that it was not worth discussing further.

And so I turned to another friend who knew of a good prospect—a maid who worked at her home named Rahda. The young woman, a

Tharu, was just the right age. After Rahda agreed to a meeting, my friend gave me photos of the prospective bride. When I showed them to Bijay, he almost swooned.

We introduced them at my house on a rainy day. Rahda was chaperoned by her boss, and I vouched for Bijay as a possible groom. As I learned, these matters must be carefully choreographed. My Nepali friends were horrified when I suggested that they might walk down the road together and have a cup of tea to get acquainted while we waited for them at my house. "They can't do that!" was the alarmed response.

After we introduced them and made some small talk, my friend and I went discreetly into an adjacent room and left them alone to get acquainted. They talked and talked and talked, until we finally had to interrupt. I learned from Bijay later that Rahda said to him at that first meeting, "I would love to eat *momos* (dumplings) made by your own hand!" Outlandish flirting, Nepali style.

They met at a public park the next Saturday, their day off, and several Saturdays after that, and chatted frequently by phone. Bijay sent her amorous text messages, which she could not read, so my friend texted back with suitably loving responses. Their romance blossomed. Bijay proposed marriage, and she accepted.

But you can't get married on any old day of your choosing in Nepal. According to tradition, a priest must read the couple's astrological charts to determine an auspicious date for the marriage to take place. I was hoping that the stars would align so I would still be in Kathmandu for their wedding. Fortunately, the gods were willing, and the date was set for a few days before my departure for the States.

But first, the groom had to buy certain gifts for the bride and her family, and vice versa. My friend did the shopping for the bride's side, and Sajani, Som's wife, shopped for Bijay. Since I had no clue what to buy or for whom, I was grateful for her help in choosing the requisite gold jewelry for the bride and appropriate gifts for her family. This was an absolute necessity, a matter of honor. It would have been humiliating for Bijay to show up for the marriage ceremony without appropriate gifts. On the wedding day, we went to a temple for an endless ceremony. The bride, groom and priest sat on the ground on carpets, and there was a lot of chanting, giving and receiving of blessings, exchanging of rings and gifts and other formalities. The groom looked a bit dazed, but very happy. The ceremony was followed by a joyful celebration in my garden that started out with a guest list of 22 and ended up with 250 people.

Several months after the wedding, James Heffelfinger, now a married man with four children, came to visit me in Kathmandu with his family, and I invited Bijay and his bride to meet with them. James and Bijay sat on the red velvet couch in my living room, chatting away, Bijay's beautiful wife at his side. They reminisced about the day, two decades earlier, when James had arrived at Kanti Hospital to deliver the medication that saved Bijay from a painful and certain death.

Ultimately, our attempts to alleviate the suffering of children at Kanti Hospital would lead to one of our foundation's most enduring and successful programs: the Nutritional Rehabilitation Homes.

CHAPTER ELEVEN

COMBATTING THE SCOURGE OF MALNUTRITION

Malnutrition is a factor in more than half the deaths of Nepali children under five, 41 percent of whom are chronically malnourished. Weakened by a vulnerable immune system, a severely malnourished child may easily contract tuberculosis or another life-threatening disease. While searching for a way to mitigate this calamity, we made a startling discovery: everything necessary to properly nourish a child is widely and inexpensively available throughout the country. The prevalence of malnutrition stemmed primarily from ignorance, rather than from poverty and a shortage of food.

During a visit to Kanti Hospital in 1997, we came across five-year-old Mina. She was suffering from a severe lung infection caused by a weakened immune system, which in turn was brought on by malnutrition. The tiny child lay shriveled on the bed, breathing with great difficulty—a sight so pitiful that it would move the most hard-hearted person to tears. She weighed only 25 pounds. Her father sat by her bedside, devastated. The doctor had just told him that Mina needed an expensive antibiotic that the hospital could not provide free of charge, and he could not afford it. We paid for the medication.

When I returned to the hospital a few days later, Mina was nowhere to be found. A nurse told me that the antibiotic had cleared up her infection, she was discharged and had returned to her village with her father. I was stunned. The child had been released even though she was in basically the same depleted condition as when she entered the hospital. She was still too weak to stand or walk unassisted and had gained only eight ounces during her stay. The nurse explained that the hospital could not afford to keep a child whose only problem was malnourishment—a common problem in Nepal—and they needed her bed for acutely ill children.

I wondered whether Mina would survive, since the underlying condition that caused her illness in the first place had not been addressed. Even if she lived, there was a good chance she would grow up physically or mentally stunted because she had returned to the same deprived environment that brought her to the hospital in the first place. Sometime later, I learned that Mina died soon after returning home. Within a few months, I heard about several other malnourished children who perished under the same circumstances.

The deaths of these children preyed on my mind. I believed they were unnecessary and that something could and must be done to prevent such tragedies. Allan and I consulted with two doctors at Kanti Hospital, Dr. Laxmi Lata, a senior pediatrician, and another young doctor who had been supported by our foundation through medical school. Together, we made a plan to open a small facility where severely malnourished children who no longer required acute medical care could be restored to health after discharge from the hospital. From the beginning, we were convinced that the only sustainable solution would be to train the mothers in the basics of good nutrition so the condition would not recur.

We rented the top floor of a children's clinic in a noisy, crowded area of Kathmandu and hired a skilled staff, including nurses, cooks, a part-time physician and one of the few academically trained dieticians in the country. Though it wasn't fancy, the three rooms were bright and clean. In February 1998, we opened the doors of the Nutritional Rehabilitation Home (NRH), ready to welcome our first little patients.

Soon, the most pitifully frail, miserable, skin-and-bones children, mostly infants and toddlers, began to show up, referred by Kanti Hospital or others who had heard about our new facility. They usually arrived in the arms of a frightened, exhausted mother, sometimes a father or another relative. Some children could not keep food down, others cried constantly and inconsolably or were almost catatonic, their heads bowed, oblivious to any stimulus. Many of them looked as though they could not survive much longer.

The families came from all areas of the country and from a variety of ethnic groups. What they had in common was a background of abject poverty, illiteracy and early marriage. Many came from rural areas where they lived in thatch-roofed huts without plumbing or electricity. It was common for the mothers to marry by the age of 16 through an arrangement between parents. In Nepali culture, a young bride moves in with her in-laws, where she is expected to obey them and do most of the household work. Often, she gives birth to a child within a year, at home, with or without a birth attendant. Shortly after her baby is born, the mother returns to her grueling schedule of daily chores in the household and in the fields.

The household hierarchy maintains that the mother-in-law rules the roost. If the baby becomes ill, she may insist on traditional remedies that are harmful to the child. For example, when a child suffers from diarrhea, she may advise her daughter-in-law not to give her any water, insisting that there is already enough liquid in her body. Medical care and information are hard to come by in rural areas. Many people hold superstitious beliefs and think that illness is the result of an evil spirit that has entered a child's body. Their first recourse is to consult a shaman, known to locals as *dhami* or *jhakri*. These are mostly elderly men, who are called upon to cure illness as well as officiate at weddings, funerals and other religious ceremonies. It is not uncommon for the shaman to order a supplicant to kill a rooster as a sacrifice to the gods before the healing ceremony begins. Then he performs an elaborate ritual: chanting, drumming, dancing and reciting incantations over and over. At the end, he pronounces the patient cured—and then he dines on the rooster.

The child's health continues to deteriorate and the mother desperately seeks another alternative. If she is fortunate enough to learn about the Nutritional Rehabilitation Home and is able to obtain permission from her mother-in-law, she will make the journey to Kathmandu. This may entail walking many miles over steep, narrow trails, carrying the child in a basket to reach the nearest road, where they can catch a bus for the long ride to the big city.

As soon as the mother and child arrive at the center, the staff jumps into action. The child is weighed and bathed, while the mother is questioned about the course of her child's illness. The patient's ragged little garments are replaced with soft, traditional Nepali baby clothes—a camisole top tied at the shoulders, pants and a long-sleeved jacket made out of flannel in the winter or the finest cotton in the summer. A doctor examines the child to be sure that her problem stems from malnutrition and that she does not have a communicable disease, and a dietician prepares a special diet based on the patient's needs. The mother is taught to feed her child tiny, nutritious meals and snacks throughout the day, and the nurses record everything the child eats and keep careful track of her progress.

Almost every day, a mother sees changes in her child as her mood, appearance and alertness improve. After a few days, the child seems to be a bit stronger and more engaged, perhaps even venturing a little smile. Within a couple of weeks, she may take a few steps and wander out to the playground to run around with the other kids. In less than a month, the large majority of children are transformed into bouncy, plump, healthy little beings.

While their children are restored to health, the mothers attend daily classes to learn the basics of proper nutrition and childcare. They gather in the kitchen for "cooking school," where they learn that simple changes in cooking and preparation can make a big difference in retaining the nutritional value of food. For example, instead of cutting and rinsing leafy greens before cooking, they are taught to wash the greens whole and steam them with the lid on to save the juices. The mothers are encouraged to feed their children vitamin A–rich yellow and orange vegetables, such as pumpkins, bananas and papayas, and to combine certain pulses and grains for maximum nutritional benefit. They learn how to prepare *jevanjel*, an oral rehydration fluid, as well as *jaolo* and *litho*, highly nutritious supplements made from locally available ingredients. There is an organic garden on the grounds where the mothers help to grow vegetables and learn about their nutritional value.

During the training, the staff clears up misconceptions held by the mothers. *Colocosia*, a huge-leafed plant that sprouts up unbidden in Nepali gardens, is used as pig feed in rural Nepal. It is rich in iron and vitamin A, and the mothers are taught to prepare it as a tasty side dish. Village wisdom dictates that young children should not be fed leafy green vegetables because they cause respiratory problems. The mothers see this is clearly not true. Most importantly, they are surprised to learn that the traditional Nepali diet of rice, lentils and vegetables is far more nutritious than the processed "fast food" they thought was better for their children. Whenever they could afford it, they splurged on cheap, processed foods such as ramen noodles, packaged cookies and soft drinks, thinking that these were more "modern," and therefore "better" than "village" food.

Training goes beyond the fundamentals of nutrition. Most of the mothers are illiterate and have little knowledge about basic childcare, such as the importance of hygiene and sanitation. Nepalis customarily eat with their hands, but are not in the habit of washing them with soap before eating. The classes cover a wide range of topics, such as the importance of boiling water before drinking, family planning, information about HIV/AIDS, and how to recognize the symptoms of serious illness.

As the children are restored to health, the mothers' health issues are also addressed. Women in rural Nepal lead lives of unremitting stress and demanding physical labor. Most of them arrive at the NRH malnourished, anemic and exhausted. Many suffer from physical maladies that the doctors are able to alleviate, such as stomach problems, fever or respiratory ailments. They gain an average of nine pounds during their stay. As the women witness their children's health improving, they begin to relax. For some, it is the first time they are able to experience the delights of motherhood. Most of them have never before had the luxury of bonding with a single child in a meaningful way.

The highlight of each day for the mothers is sitting on straw mats on the terrace, gossiping and playing with the children. The nurses move among them with compassionate authority, gently patting a child on the cheek, asking the mothers about their food preferences and answering their questions. As the sun breaks through the fog and warms the terrace, the mothers remove their babies' clothing, slather mustard oil on their little bodies and massage them gently. Oil massage for babies is a time-honored tradition among Nepali women, the very incarnation of hands-on motherly love.

As they bask in the sun, the mothers talk about their lives and the circumstances that brought them to the nutrition center. On a recent morning, a 15 year-old mother, who was cradling a young toddler in her lap, said they had come from a rock-breaking camp along a river in the Dhading District, to the west of Kathmandu. The rock-breaking business supplies the Nepali construction industry's insatiable demand for gravel. Work at these camps is among the most dangerous and lowest paid jobs in the country and the workers come from some of Nepal's poorest families, invariably illiterate and landless. They live in simple shelters—nothing more than straw huts. As men pry large rocks from the riverbed with iron bars and pickaxes, the women, often with their children, sit on the bare ground, totally unprotected from flying shards. All day long, they pound large rocks into gravel with small sledgehammers. Sanitation is nonexistent.

The mother explained that her baby had started crawling and

seemed to be developing well when she noticed abnormal swelling in her hands and feet. She thought the swelling might have been her mother-in-law's fault because she swaddled the baby too tightly in blankets. When the baby's condition became more severe, she and her husband took her to Kanti Hospital. Five days later, they were referred to the Nutritional Rehabilitation Home, where the baby was nursed back to health. Swelling in the extremities is a classic symptom of a type of malnutrition called *kwashiorkor* that is caused by protein deficiency. Over the years, many children at our center have recovered from this life-threatening condition.

Another mother proudly told the women on the terrace that her 18 month-old son had gained six pounds since their arrival two weeks earlier. He had been so desperately ill—near death—that a meddling neighbor in her village had said, "I'll cut off my ear if your baby survives." The neighbor was in for a surprise!

In less than a month, almost all the children reach a normal weight for their age and are strong enough to make the journey home. During the training, the mothers are encouraged to share the knowledge they have gained about nutrition and childcare with other women in their village.

To assure that the children continue to thrive, we send field workers to check on their health after discharge, often requiring them to walk for hours on rugged trails to reach a child's village. The field workers carry a simple scale. If they find that a child is losing weight or is having other problems, they remind the mother of the basic principles of good nutrition and urge her to put into practice what she learned at the NRH. In case the condition poses a serious health risk, the field worker urges the mother to bring the child back to the center.

Over the years, the field workers have found that almost all the mothers have learned their lessons well and their children were thriving. Many of them proudly teach "cooking classes" and share their newfound knowledge with neighbors. Having seen with their own eyes the dramatic changes in desperately ill children who were cared for at the nutrition center and returned home plump and healthy, other mothers in the village are eager to learn how to feed and care for their children.

It was thrilling to see the dramatic improvement in the health of the few hundred children who were fortunate enough to come to the nutrition center in Kathmandu, but with limited bed space available at a single facility, we were not having enough of an impact on the larger problem of child malnutrition throughout the country. More than 75 percent of Nepalis live in rural areas, and many families did not know about the center or could not afford to bring a malnourished child to Kathmandu. We needed to do more.

Three years after we opened our first nutrition center, an official of the United Nation's World Health Organization heard about the facility during a trip to Nepal and asked the Ministry of Health to arrange a visit. The Ministry sent one of its officers to accompany him, and together they toured the facility. After examining the medical records of the children who had been rehabilitated there, the United Nations representative turned to his Nepali companion and said, "This is what the Nepal government should be doing all over the country. Why not build a facility like this on the site of every zonal hospital?" "Great idea," agreed the Nepali official. He turned to our manager standing beside him and asked the Nepali equivalent of, "How about it?"

Som and I discussed the matter and decided to bring the issue to our board. Nepal is divided into 14 zones, and each has a central hospital supported by the government. It would be an ambitious undertaking for a small nonprofit like ours to build a center at each of these hospitals, but we were convinced that if we succeeded, we could make a significant contribution toward ending child malnutrition in Nepal.

There was a catch, however. We did not want to assume responsibility for the satellite facilities in perpetuity. At the same time, the administrators of some of the zonal hospitals were reluctant to allow us to build the centers on the hospital premises because they were concerned that we might withdraw our support at some time in the future and they would be left with the responsibility for continuing the program. After much back-and-forth between the foundation, the Ministry of Health and the hospitals themselves, we came up with a solution. Our foundation would build a Nutritional Rehabilitation Home close to each zonal hospital's pediatric ward, hire and train the staff and operate the program for three years, paying all expenses. In the fourth and fifth years, the hospital would share operating costs with the foundation. After that, the hospital would assume full responsibility for operations and expenses. The Ministry of Health agreed to incorporate the costs of operating the centers into each zonal hospital's budget as it resumed responsibility for operations.

Skeptics familiar with how things run in Nepal warned us that the government would not fulfill its promise of support. Some had experienced disappointment with commitments made by the Nepali government, and told us, "Yeah, yeah, we'll see."

In 2003, we built the first outlying nutrition center in Nepalgunj, an area with many malnourished children. Over the next 10 years, our foundation constructed 16 NRHs throughout the country, exceeding our goal, because two of the larger zones needed more than one facility. Each center has 10 beds, except Nepalgunj, which has 17. By 2013, eight of the zonal hospitals had assumed full responsibility for funding and operations. We anticipate that all the Nutritional Rehabilitation Homes will be turned over to the government by the end of 2018. The foundation continues to monitor and provide technical support to these satellite facilities, and so far the transition has been smooth. The hospitals have retained the staff members we recruited and trained, and the Ministry of Health has allocated a sufficient budget for their continued operations.

Following the success of the nutrition center satellite program, we decided to expand the mission of the NRH in Kathmandu to disseminating throughout Nepal the knowledge we had gained over 15 years about the rehabilitation of malnourished children. Prevention is a more effective strategy than intervention. We wanted to create new programs that would bring awareness of good nutritional practices to families, as well as to workers who planned meals at hospitals and other institutions around the country.

But to do so, we needed a larger, more suitable physical facility. Ever since we opened the first center in Kathmandu in 1998, it had been housed in quarters inappropriate for its purpose. The first center was on the top floor of a building in a crowded, polluted part of the city, without suitable play areas for the children. Later, we moved to a rented building meant for a family, where the rooms were too small for the number of beds required. We had to build crude structures for additional beds, and a dining hall. The water supply was unreliable. When we needed space to train nutrition workers or hold a meeting, we had to kick the kids out of their playroom, which was a problem, especially during monsoon season. The building was in a residential area, and the neighbors complained about the noise of crying children.

After several years of rattling our begging bowls, we raised the money to purchase land and construct a building suited to our needs. In 2008, we bought a small plot on a little knoll about 15 minutes from Kathmandu. It overlooks green rice fields, has a beautiful view of the mountains and is free of the toxic pollution that engulfs the city. We built an attractive, light-filled structure with ample room for 24 beds, a large training hall with a library, a spacious kitchen where mothers can gather for cooking classes, an organic vegetable garden and several terraces for the women to lounge in the sun with their babies on winter mornings. And, of course, there is a playroom and playground for the children so they have an outlet for their energy as their health improves.

Our goal is to make this flagship facility the center for nutrition education, rehabilitation and training for all of Nepal.

The new center has helped in our quest to spread the word about good nutritional practices. Our staff provides consultation services to institutions throughout Nepal that are engaged in preparing meals for their residents, such as monasteries, boarding schools, hospitals and children's homes. If, as sometimes happens, children from these institutions are admitted to our program suffering from malnutrition, the staff volunteers to visit the organization and advise those involved in food preparation about hygiene and good nutrition practices.

We also conduct training courses for "barefoot dieticians," who are responsible for planning diets and preparing food at government hospitals. The hospitals provide free food to their patients, but it is notoriously unappetizing, low in nutritional value and prepared in an unhygienic environment. There are only a handful of academically trained dieticians in the country, including the dietician who has been with our center from the beginning. To alleviate this shortage, we provide the same training to the "barefoot dieticians" as for the staff of the outlying NRH facilities.

We have also expanded the program to provide nutrition education for families living in rural areas. Our staff travels to communities around the country to conduct "nutrition camps" in a school or government building, in coordination with local government agencies. Some camps are held in areas so remote that porters are needed to carry the equipment to the location. Prior to each camp, the community receives notice through leaflets, FM radio broadcasts and word of mouth that doctors, nurses and other medical personnel will be coming to the area to offer medical care for malnourished children, as well as advice for mothers. Often, mothers will walk with their children for many hours, their feet clad in plastic flip-flops, to reach a camp.

When our staff arrives, hundreds of people are waiting, milling around. Some of the mothers have five or six children in tow—one in a basket carried on her back, another in her arms, the rest trailing along behind her. The mothers line up patiently, waiting their turn, while the toddlers play on the sidelines. The camp is organized into stations. First, the mothers and their children waiting in line are given hand-washing lessons. The staff then registers the children, records their health history, weighs them, measures their height and assesses their nutritional status. Children with medical problems are examined by a doctor and given medication, if needed. The staff provides the mothers with a condensed version of "Nutrition 101." They are taught how to prepare *"litho,"* a tasty, nutritious supplement made of local ingredients and, to the delight of the children, are given a supply to take home. At some camps, half of the children are found to be malnourished or suffering from infections.

If a child is severely malnourished, the mother is advised to take her to the nearest nutrition center. It is not uncommon for a family to be so poor that they cannot afford the bus fare. When this happens, we pay the cost of transportation. Occasionally, so many children need hospitalization that the closest facility cannot accommodate them all, so we bring a whole busload of malnourished children and their mothers to the facility in Kathmandu.

Medical care in rural Nepal is so scarce that many adults come to the camps seeking help for eye problems, orthopedic issues, and other afflictions when they learn that a doctor will be present, even though they know that the camp is meant for malnourished children. It is impossible to treat them without depriving the children at the camp of the care they need, so we refer these adults to other organizations. Our experience at the nutrition camps reveals the alarming lack of health care and nutritional knowledge in remote areas of Nepal. There is much left to do.

Since the first Nutritional Rehabilitation Home opened in 1998, over 15,000 children have been restored to health and their mothers educated about good nutrition practices. The cost is only $260 for an average of one month of hospitalization and training for the mother. Our follow-up studies show that over 93 percent of the children discharged from the facility have maintained a healthy weight.

One of my favorite things in life is to visit the nutrition centers. It is thrilling beyond words to see toddlers who had arrived just a few weeks earlier in the most pathetic condition with their exhausted mothers, ready to be discharged. The children are in blooming good health, and their mothers are rested, well nourished and armed with knowledge about how to take better care of their kids. Sometimes, as I leave, I think to myself, "Little Mina, you did not die in vain."

CHAPTER TWELVE

ANCIENT ROOTS OF INJUSTICE

I have never forgotten the shame and embarrassment I experienced more than 70 years ago when an elderly black man in a small town in Mississippi felt obliged to step into the gutter to address me because I was a white woman. Since then, and through all the years I worked on civil rights issues as a lawyer at the California Supreme Court and closely followed the movement for the rights of black people, the plight of the oppressed and the exploited has concerned me deeply. Many years later, thousands of miles from home, in a radically different cultural setting, I was able to work through the Nepal Youth Foundation to empower, educate and improve the lives of two of the most subjugated and abused populations of Nepal: girls and members of the Dalit caste.

It is difficult to imagine a more repressive, unjust, cruel stratification of society than the caste system. The populace is rigidly divided into high and low castes, with Dalits, or "untouchables," at the bottom. Membership in a caste is hereditary and permanent, and so deeply entrenched in Nepali society that it has persisted since ancient times. Although the Nepali government formally outlawed caste discrimination in the 1960s, the practice endures, particularly in rural communities, where over 75 percent of Nepali people live.

Relegated to the very bottom rung of society, Dalits are considered by the rest of society to be "impure" and "polluted." They are forced into hereditary, caste-based occupations denoting low social status—tailor, blacksmith, shoemaker, basket weaver, potter, musician, entertainer. Some Dalits are destined to sweep streets, some to clean toilets and some to work as scavengers, discarding carcasses of dead livestock.

They have suffered centuries of social exclusion, discrimination, food shortages, lack of education and violence. Estimates of the number of Dalits living in Nepal vary greatly. According to the 2011 national census, they make up 13.6 percent of the total population (approximately 3.6 million people). Most Dalits earn less than $1 a day. Child and maternal mortality rates are higher for Dalits than for the general population, and life expectancy is lower. Land ownership is a major indicator of status and security in Nepal, and few Dalits own land sufficient to support a family's survival.

Strict customs govern the relationship between the castes. Physical contact is frowned upon for fear of spiritual pollution. As a result, Dalits are sometimes denied access to temples and communal water taps. The women are vulnerable to sexual exploitation and charges of witchcraft, and marriage between the castes is a serious offense to society. Inter-caste couples who do marry are shunned by their families and communities. Dalits rarely move forward to higher education or professional careers in business or politics.

How could we even begin to mitigate a problem of such enormous cultural, social and economic magnitude? Although we knew that any efforts we would make to improve the lives of Dalits would have limited impact, we decided to give it a try.

Our first project was a daycare center for the children of women who swept the streets of Kathmandu. From the moment I first set foot in the city, I was horrified at the sight of women with long-handled straw brooms sweeping the filthy streets, with babies strapped on their backs or toddlers crawling along behind them. The children and their mothers were enveloped in clouds of dust and black exhaust that spewed from the vehicles on the clogged roadways. Many adults in Kathmandu develop respiratory problems from breathing the foul air for the few hours they are out on the street. I could only imagine what damage such pollution was doing to the respiratory tracts of infants. As I watched these tiny children inhaling the poisoned air, I thought to myself, "There must be some way to get those babies off their mothers' backs!"

The sweeper women were Dalits, and sweeping was their caste occupation. They lived with their families in a small, constricted neighborhood in Kathmandu with about 1,500 members of their caste, crowded into ramshackle huts with pigs and chickens roaming freely among the open sewers and muddy alleys.

We decided to open a shelter to care for children during the day while their mothers swept the streets. Realizing that we needed someone to reach out to the community on our behalf, we turned to Tika Basnet, a Nepali friend and committed social worker. She approached a number of families in the community and asked if they would be interested in having their children cared for during the day while they worked. At first, the families were unsure if they wanted strangers looking after their sons and daughters, but after some hesitation, they embraced the idea. In 1990, we rented a small house in the neighborhood, furnished it, and trained some of the women in the community to be caretakers, managers and teachers for 32 young children. Each morning, the mothers dropped off their infants and toddlers at the center, where they received nutritious food, medical care, clothing, some education and loving supervision throughout the day. The parents paid the equivalent of a few cents a week.

From the beginning, we made it clear that we would provide full support for only five years. Thereafter, the families would have to come up with a way to maintain the center, at least partially. We hoped that some of the mothers would volunteer to reduce the operating costs or that they would pay a higher fee, so they would not rely on us completely for support. Despite our encouragement, the community's participation was minimal and we saw no signs of progress toward sustainability. As the center was approaching the end of its fourth year, a wondrous thing happened.

While Allan and I were in the United States, we received word that the city of Kathmandu, which employed the sweepers, had approached our manager and asked to take over full support of the center. They planned to use it as a model to establish similar facilities in other sweeper communities. This was the ideal outcome. As with many projects in developing countries, the hope is that if an aid agency creates a successful model, the government or local community will eventually take responsibility for running it. The center was handed over to the city in an elaborate ceremony, with glowing speeches by the mayor about its past and future.

When I returned to Nepal several months later, the daycare center was gone. Despite promises made by city officials, once they took over operations, they failed to pay the rent or salaries. There was no alternative but to close it down. We were heartsick, but decided not to revive the project. The building where the center was located was no longer available, there was no suitable place within the neighborhood to open another facility, and because of caste discrimination, it was impossible to rent quarters outside the community's boundaries. We would have to be content that for five years, 32 young children received excellent care and did not have to spend their days on the foul streets of Kathmandu.

The Nepal Youth Foundation's scholarship program had provided a pathway out of poverty for hundreds of impoverished and disabled Nepali children. We talked it over and decided that perhaps the best way to help the Dalit community would be to focus our efforts on education. Dalit students faced serious obstacles to attending school. Some parents could not pay even the minimal cost for a uniform and supplies. Those who did enroll often suffered segregation and discrimination, including harassment and insults from students of higher castes. Even some teachers treated them with disdain, forcing them to stand at the back of the classroom and refusing to answer their questions. Occasionally, teachers would not even touch a Dalit's homework, compelling the child to sit on the floor and turn the pages for review.

We wanted to open a school where Dalit children would feel welcome and receive a superior education, not only for the sake of their own advancement, but to demonstrate to others that Dalits were fully capable of excelling in school and in life. With thousands of Dalit settlements throughout Nepal, we were unsure where to build, but we soon stumbled upon a community that was a good prospect. NYF had recently expanded its scholarship program to the Dhading District, 70 miles northwest of Kathmandu, and we were sponsoring several hundred students in local schools.

One of Som's jobs as program officer for our foundation was to visit the schools, meet with the students and their teachers, check on their academic progress and distribute scholarship funds. He spent many long days walking along the trails in remote areas without roads or electricity. Along the way, he came across a number of government schools, all in abysmal condition. They were housed in dilapidated buildings, some on the verge of collapse, with no toilets or running water, often with no windows or ventilation. There was a scarcity of both schools and teachers.

One day in 1999, Som and Nabin, a local teacher, were walking along a trail in Dhading when they came across a Dalit settlement. It was a small community of blacksmiths, with about 65 households. The inhabitants lived in tiny thatch-roofed huts perched on steep, narrow terraces. Som and Nabin stopped for a cup of tea and struck up a conversation with the locals. The villagers told them that most Dalit children started at the local primary school, but 90 percent of them dropped out early. Not a single child in the community had made it through 5th grade. They ended up as farm or factory laborers, or workers in a nearby slate mine. Some landed on the streets of Kathmandu, homeless and destitute.

We decided to build a school near the blacksmith community where Dalit students would feel at home. But we didn't want to build just any school—and not just for Dalits. We hoped to build a school so outstanding that parents of higher castes would clamor to enroll their children. We would create a model for educational excellence that would promote reverse segregation.

Right about that time, we received a generous offer from the Yokohama International School in Japan to fund the construction of a school in Nepal at a place of our choosing. Three local farmers, all members of higher castes, donated one and a half acres of land and the villagers provided sweat equity for the construction. For 15 months, Dalits and non-Dalits worked side by side, performing backbreaking labor to build the school. After leveling terraces to prepare a flat, open space, they quarried stone, transported it to the site and constructed walls on a solid foundation. The chief contractor was a Dalit man whose son was one of the first students at the school. This brilliant young man passed the college entrance examination with distinction several years later.

While the building was under construction, staff members from our foundation visited Dalit and non-Dalit communities in the area to convince parents that their children would receive a good education at the new school. "The parents wanted their kids to be educated," says Som, "but understandably, they had lost faith in government schools that were staffed with untrained, unmotivated teachers. But when we told the parents that we were going to build an outstanding school to educate Dalit children, as well as others from higher castes, it was an easy sell."

In August 2000, the new school opened its doors to 130 students in kindergarten and 1st and 2nd grades, with scholarships provided for all Dalit children. We recruited local teachers and gave them extensive training in early childhood and primary education. The villagers and the Yokohama International School chose the name Sunaula Chowa, the "Golden Harmony School." *Sunaula* means "golden" in Nepali and *chowa* means "harmony" in Japanese.

Rita was one of the first students to enroll at Sunaula Chowa. She recalls, "When they were building the new school, I stopped by to watch the progress every day. I was seven years old and I thought it was the most beautiful building I had ever seen. It had big windows all around, running water and even a real bathroom. There were benches and desks, so no one would have to sit on the floor. Best of all, there was a playground with swings and slides. I had never seen such a thing before. With all my heart, I wanted to study at that school."

But there was a rumor in the community that only one child from a household would be admitted. Rita begged her parents to send her to the school, but they told her, "If we are forced to choose just one child, we will send your brother." Even now, many years later, Rita recalls the disappointment she felt when her parents told her that she could not go to school because she was a girl. But then she learned that this was not true—all children in a family could enroll and Dalit girls in particular were welcome.

When Sunaula Chowa opened in 2000, most of the students were Dalits, but as the school added higher grades and more students, Dalits became a minority. As we had hoped, when parents of higher castes realized the school was better than any other in the area, they were eager to enroll their children. The school expanded each year until enrollment reached 500 students in kindergarten through 10th grade.

Sunaula Chowa has established itself as the best school in the entire Dhading District. In the past six years, over 100 students have graduated and passed the college entrance exam, almost all with extremely high grades. Only the very best private schools in Kathmandu can boast similar results.

From the beginning, we planned to turn Sunaula Chowa over to the community once the school was up and running. To enable the villagers to support the school and continue to provide scholarships, we purchased an adjoining plot of land so they could cultivate crops for sale. They grow bananas and pineapples for the local market and are raising goats in the community forest nearby to generate income.

In 2010, Sunaula Chowa merged with a local public school and is now supported by the community, supplemented by funding from the Nepali government. Whenever the subject of fees arises, Dalit parents flex their muscles and remind the administration that the school was established for them and that their children must continue to receive full scholarships. "We're not paying," they insist. "This is OUR school."

Rita graduated from 10th grade and passed the college entrance examinations with distinction—a level achieved by only a small percentage of the half-million Nepali students who take the test each year. She was awarded a full scholarship to Polytechnic College in Kathmandu and graduated first in her class. She is currently working as a health assistant at the Kathmandu Nutritional Rehabilitation Home.

"I am very proud to be the first girl to graduate from college in my village," Rita said. "I plan to enter medical school to become a doctor so I can provide health care to the Dalit community."

"Educating a girl is like watering your neighbor's garden." This loathsome saying embodies the reality of life for the majority of girls growing up in rural Nepal, who suffer discrimination and domination from the time they are born. Subjugation of women occurs despite the fact that there is irrefutable evidence that empowering girls and women in developing countries reaps the greatest rewards for society. It yields the highest return of any development investment not only for the individual, but also for families and society as a whole. An education empowers women to overcome poverty and achieve financial independence. They are more likely to marry later, utilize family planning and send their own daughters to school. An educated woman is better equipped to become a decision-maker in her family and community, and to resist exploitation, political extremism, violence and abuse.

There is great joy and celebration in Nepali villages when a boy is born, but the arrival of a baby girl is greeted with far less enthusiasm and sometimes with outright sadness, disappointment and even rejection. In many Nepali families, boys receive preferential treatment when it comes to education, nutrition, health care and career opportunities.

A girl is dominated by men throughout her life, first by her father and brothers, and later by her husband and sons. After an arranged marriage, she is considered to be her husband's property and must live with and serve her spouse and his family. A married woman spends her days doing housework—cooking, cleaning, washing, providing elder care, and, in rural areas, working in the fields. Someday, if she's lucky and has a son who gets married, she will rule the roost and lord it over her own daughter-in-law.

In 2004, we began giving scholarships to girls who lived in Kavre, Gorkha, Dhading and Nuwakot, most of them Dalits. Many girls in these rural districts enrolled in school, but the majority dropped out by 4th or 5th grade. Our goal was to stem the dropout rate and prevent early marriage. We knew from experience that providing scholarships in rural Nepal has a domino effect. Once a substantial number of students in an area enroll in school, other children badger their parents to let them join their friends.

Eventually, 500 girls in the four districts received scholarships to local schools. We kept a close watch on them once they were enrolled to make sure they did not drop out. Our field workers visited the schools regularly to check on the children and discuss problems with the headmasters and students. There was constant tension with families who wanted to marry the girls off so they would no longer have to support them. Many of these students have graduated from 10th grade and gone on to college or vocational training. As we had hoped, the dropout rate in the districts has decreased dramatically, as has the rate of early marriage.

We were pleased with the progress of the girls' scholarship program, but we realized that it would be a long time before most of these youngsters finished their education, and we wanted to have a more immediate impact on the lives of Dalit women. In 2006, a Dalit men's organization approached us and suggested that we create a college scholarship program for talented Dalit girls with leadership potential. Few Dalit girls went on to higher education, and we jumped at the opportunity. We created a new program called "Empowering Dalit Daughters." The goal was to provide opportunities for smart, ambitious young Dalit women to achieve personal and professional success so they would become leaders and role models within and outside their communities. We placed ads in newspapers throughout Nepal, encouraging Dalit girls who had passed the college entrance exams to apply. Beyond academic excellence, we were looking for girls who were enterprising, energetic and above all, ardent champions for the cause of Dalit empowerment. After an extensive application and interview process, 24 young women were invited to join the college program.

We rented a hostel in Kathmandu where the girls could live together while attending private colleges in the city. At first, it was a challenging time for them all. Most had never ventured far from their villages and they were bewildered, anxious and intimidated by the crowds and chaos of the city. They had lived in small shelters with their families, and now they shared a large house with 23 other girls from diverse ethnic groups who came from all over the country. Despite their differences, they shared a common bond: all were fiercely determined to get an education and to fight against the oppression and humiliation of Dalits.

When I first met them, I was stunned that these smart, lively, attractive and dynamic young women were classified as "untouchables." They were nicely dressed in traditional Nepali style, well groomed, and shy, but well spoken. Most of them were beautiful as well. What moved and impressed me the most was the way they so quickly developed warm and supportive relationships with one another. There can be few cultures in the world in which a group of teenage girls from diverse ethnic groups, all from oppressed minorities, could bond so quickly. They became the closest of friends, helping each other academically and personally. As the hostel became a safe, nurturing home for them, it seemed like a K House for Dalit college students.

Sarita was one of the first girls to be selected for the Empowering Dalit Daughters program. Just months after she was born, her father abandoned her 16 year-old mother. Destitute, and with no way to earn a living, her mother decided to move to her brother's home. Carrying tiny Sarita in a basket on her back, she walked to a small village in the Rautahat District, where they moved in with Sarita's uncle. He was a schoolteacher, one of the few educated Dalits in Nepal at the time. When Sarita was five, her uncle enrolled her in kindergarten at the local public school. He kept a careful eye on her progress, tutoring her at home and encouraging her to excel. She did her homework by the light of a kerosene lantern and often stayed up studying long after midnight.

"When I was around 11 and 12," Sarita recalls, "I felt ashamed of being a Dalit, even though I did not really understand what that meant. I was discriminated against by my classmates and other villagers." Occasionally, teachers ignored her and would not answer her questions. She and other Dalits were forced to stand at the back of the line at the public water tap and wait until people of higher castes were finished. Whenever Sarita and her friends stopped for a cup of tea, she had to remain outside the teahouse while her higher caste friends sat inside. Then she had to wash her own cup to purify it.

After she graduated from high school with honors, Sarita responded to an ad in a local newspaper about the Empowering Dalit Daughters program. Following a long interview, she was invited to join. As Sarita and the other girls adjusted to life in an unfamiliar environment, the language barrier presented a big challenge. They were enrolled in excellent private colleges in Kathmandu, where the classes were conducted in English. Since they had come from rural government schools, their English was not up to the task. They found it daunting at first, but with extra tutoring and practice, they became fluent in English in a surprisingly short time.

"I was homesick when I first came to the hostel in Kathmandu," Sarita remembers. "I missed my mother and uncle very much. But when I discovered that I had 23 new sisters at the hostel, I was lonely no more."

Sarita and the other girls were exposed to a broad spectrum of opportunities in diverse fields, including business, hotel management, public health, social work, technology, journalism and medicine. Field trips throughout Nepal opened their eyes to life in communities beyond Kathmandu and their own villages. The girls participated in rallies and debates about economic, social and political issues; they learned to stand up for their rights as Dalits and as women, and to speak out against exclusion, gender bias and violence against women. During school breaks, they worked as interns for various media outlets and social organizations, where they honed their management and communication skills. For several months, Sarita worked as an intern at the U.S. Agency for International Development in Kathmandu.

All the young women in the Empowering Dalit Daughters program have graduated from college and are forging their own paths in the world. Two have received scholarships to medical school. These smart young women will be the first doctors in their caste and plan to go back to their communities to practice medicine. Several graduates are working part-time while studying for master's degrees in journalism, sociology and conflict management. One was chosen out of 500 applicants to work at the American Embassy in Kathmandu. Others are employed as social workers; one of the graduates works for an an organization in Kathmandu that fights sex trafficking and physical abuse of women and children. Two are pursuing careers in the hotel industry.

These bright, savvy, ambitious young women are shining examples of what a Dalit woman can achieve. Although they come from the most oppressed, marginalized and despised group in Nepali society, they have become confident, competent professionals. They are highly aware of issues of inclusion and equal access, and have become vocal advocates against injustice.

The Empowering Dalit Daughters project has had a surprising social impact. Our graduates tell us that the attitude of members of the upper castes toward the girls and their families has changed to one of respect and friendliness. Parents of our graduates are invited to participate in community events, a rare occurrence before their daughters were educated. As other Dalit families observe the transformation and success of these young women, they encourage their own daughters to stay in school. This project has not only developed leaders in the Dalit community, but has enhanced social inclusion in Nepali society as well.

Sarita graduated from Kathmandu Model College in 2009 with a major in English and mass communication. She married a founder of the Dalit men's organization that had suggested the Empowering Dalit Daughters program to our foundation, and they have two young children. In spite of these responsibilities, she has worked part time as a translator for western filmmakers reporting on the kamlari issue, and is pursuing a master's degree in journalism.

The young woman who not so long ago was barred from entering a teahouse with her friends because she is a Dalit, says, "I want to let people know girls can be anything—a journalist, a lawyer, a businesswoman—and I want to help people who have been oppressed understand their rights. I feel like a leader now. I can go to my village and express my feelings. I can speak for my rights. I can speak for my community's rights. I can be an example. I am an empowered woman."

The house where Som grew up in Gorkha

Som and Preb Stritter, thirty-three years after he was her student

Dilapidated government school

Classroom at a government school

Another rundown schoolroom

Studying outdoors for lack of a classroom

A cowshed used as a classroom

School building that replaced the cowshed

Bandevi School, close to collapse

New school constructed in its place

Som and Sajani

Bride and groom with matchmaker

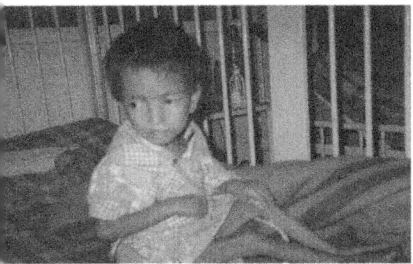
Little Mina, whose death inspired the creation of the Nutritional Rehabilitation Homes

Mothers learning about nutrition

Mothers tending the vegetable garden

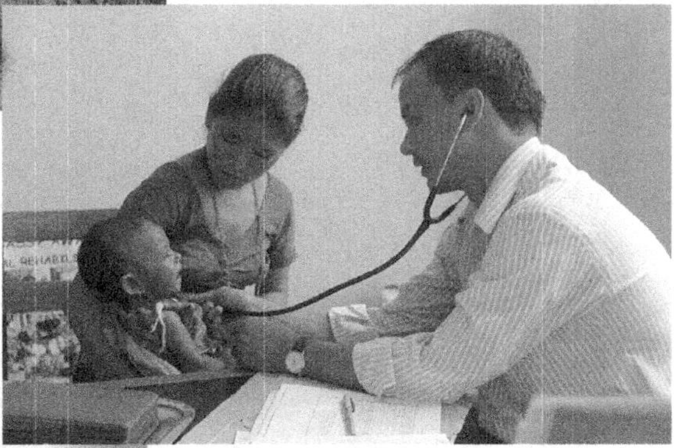

Doctor examining baby for admission

Visiting the Nutritional Rehabilitation Home

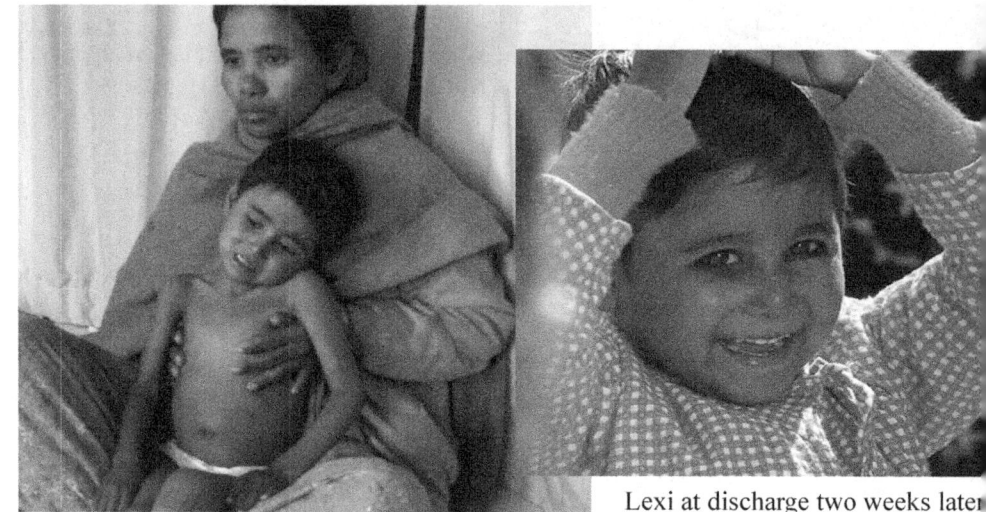

Lexi at admission

Lexi at discharge two weeks later

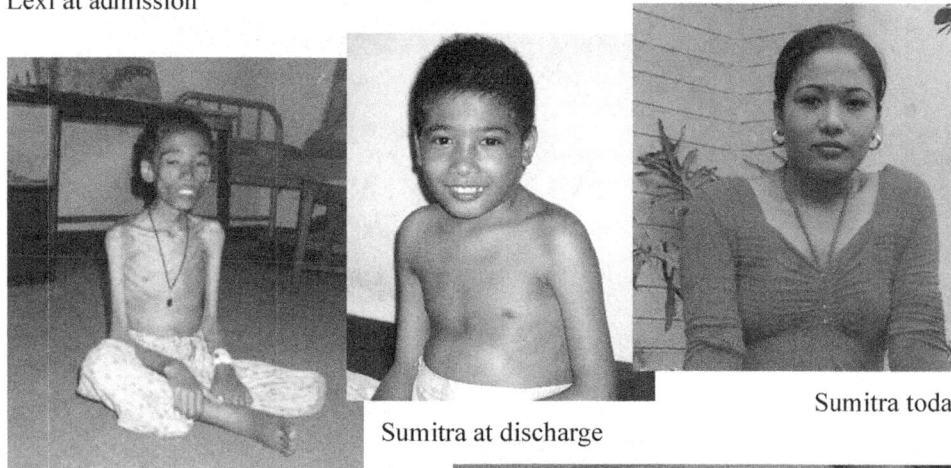

Sumitra at admission

Sumitra at discharge

Sumitra today

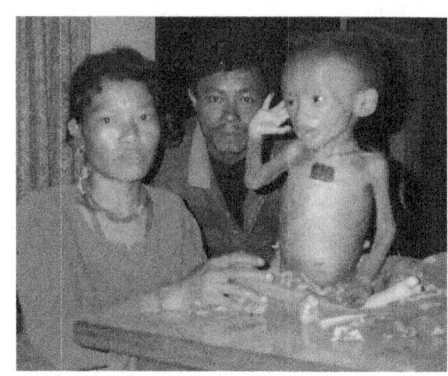

Dinesh at admission

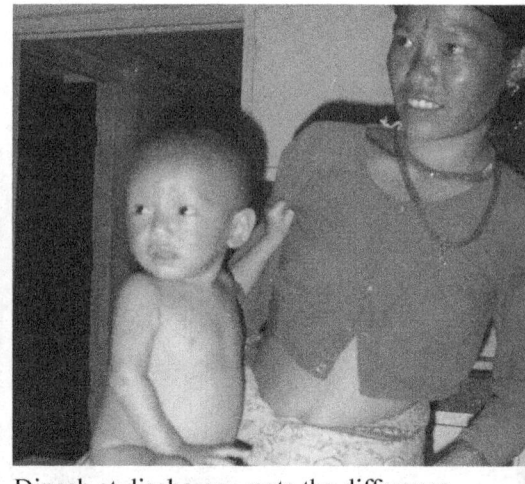

Dinesh at discharge - note the difference in his mother's appearance

Beautiful, modern Nutritional
Rehabilitation Home
in Kathmandu

Standing in line at nutrition camp

Sunaula Chowa, the Golden
Harmony School

Girls at government school in tattered uniforms

Here they are with new uniforms, book bags and shoes

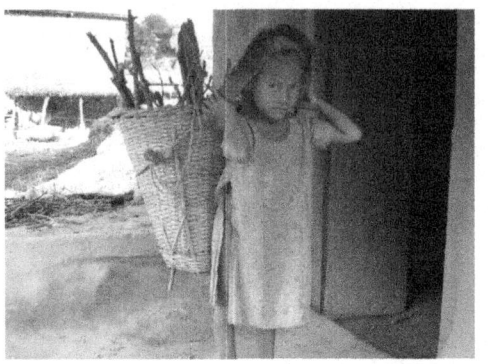

And later in her school uniform

Karuna, before we gave her a scholarship

Empowering Dalit Daughters program

Dalit college girls in my garden in Kathmandu

CHAPTER THIRTEEN

GIRL POWER

To the annoyance of morning commuters, a curious thing was happening on the streets of downtown Kathmandu on January 6, 2009. The roads were clogged with hundreds of young women decked out in colorful traditional dresses. They brought traffic to a standstill as they marched through the streets, carrying signs and distributing leaflets to passersby. With fists raised high in the air, the girls chanted, "Stop selling daughters! End the kamlari system!" The young women were former Kamlaris who had traveled hundreds of miles by bus from the Dang District to reach Kathmandu that morning.

The girls slept fitfully the night before the journey, worried about what the next day would bring. Some had never been to Kathmandu, but had heard that the city was enormous, noisy and chaotic. Others were returning to the city for the first time since they had been freed from bondage and were excited to be coming back as empowered young women demanding their rights. They wondered how people would react to 400 girls marching through the streets to demonstrate against the kamlari practice.

Rising before dawn, they donned their long-skirted green and red Tharu costumes, said goodbye to their families and proceeded to the bus station, where hundreds of liberated Kamlaris gathered for the journey to Kathmandu. It was a cold, foggy morning. They shivered in their thin shawls as the rickety busses revved up their motors and headed for the big city. None of the young women who boarded the bus that morning realized that they were completing a journey that began years before at a British university and eventually wended its way to the Supreme Court of Nepal.

In 2002, Som was awarded a prestigious scholarship to the University of East Anglia in Norwich, England, to study for a master's degree in International Child Welfare, and the foundation granted him a leave of absence to pursue his studies. He chose the kamlari practice as the topic for his thesis. While researching the laws relating to child protection, he learned that the practice of indenturing children to work as laborers violated not only the general laws of Nepal regulating labor, but also 22 of the 42 articles of the United Nations Convention on the Rights of the Child, to which Nepal was a signatory.

When Som returned to Kathmandu, his master's degree (with distinction) in hand, he brought an action in the Supreme Court of Nepal seeking an order to force the government to comply with these laws. In a landmark decision in 2006, the Court held that the kamlari practice was a violation of both Nepali and international law. It ordered the government to provide rehabilitation services to the girls who had returned from servitude.

At the time the decision was handed down, Nepal was just emerging from a 10-year Maoist insurgency. Enforcement of the law was feeble at best, even during more tranquil times, so it was not surprising that the government made no attempt to implement the Supreme Court's decision. Nevertheless, the decision had some beneficial effects. Advocates waved it under the noses of recalcitrant employers who balked at releasing their bonded servants, and cited it to judges in the many lawsuits our foundation brought to force employers to comply with the law.

But these victories were small potatoes compared to the urgency of liberating thousands of girls still living in servitude. Despite our success in rescuing over 3,500 Kamlaris, we were disheartened, knowing that over 10,000 remained in bondage. We knew that we could free them and end the kamlari custom forever, if only we had the money. The problem was that we were resolved to provide education or vocational training to all the girls we liberated, but we couldn't afford the cost of rehabilitating 10,000 additional Kamlaris. After much hand wringing, we came up with an idea—why not get the Nepali government to ante up? Maybe we could dust off the Supreme Court's 2006 decision outlawing the kamlari practice and compel the government to follow the order to provide rehabilitation services for the returned girls.

In 2009, we mounted a campaign to pressure the central government to do just that. It was an ideal time for such an effort. Following the end of the Maoist insurgency, human rights violations committed during the conflict were on everybody's mind. Kathmandu was awash with civil society groups and international organizations eager to investigate and correct such violations.

Man Bahadur, the champion of the Kamlaris, made arrangements for the 400 former Kamlaris to make the 14-hour bus ride from Dang to Kathmandu, in the hope of capturing the attention of the central government. The girls marched through the city streets carrying banners, distributing leaflets, chanting anti-bonding slogans and performing street plays along the way. There was extensive radio and television coverage of the event. We arranged for a delegation of the girls to meet with high-ranking government officials, including the president, the prime minister, the United Nations human rights commissioner, members of Parliament and leaders of the major political parties. The girls warned the officials that they would spread their protest throughout the country if the government ignored their plight.

Reaching out through the media to a broad national audience, they spoke powerfully and emotionally about their childhoods as bonded servants and the inhumanity of the kamlari practice. By the time they left Kathmandu five days later, neither the *thulo manchhes* (big shots) in government nor the general public could turn a blind eye to the kamlari issue. There was a national call demanding that the government take action on their behalf.

As a result, in July 2009 the Parliament appropriated $1.6 million in its budget for the education and rehabilitation of formerly bonded girls—an enormous sum in Nepal. In later years, it made even larger appropriations for this purpose. The Ministry of Education appointed our foundation as its chief advisor in implementing the government's rehabilitation efforts. We would continue to rescue the remaining Kamlaris and carry out the anti-bonding campaign, while the government would pay for the education and rehabilitation of the returned girls.

To my delight, the Ministry accepted our advice to use some of the appropriated funds to support school hostels for girls who had no home to return to because they were orphans or their families could not care for them. I had spent many sleepless nights worrying about little girls condemned to spending their childhoods in labor bondage because they did not have families who could support them if they were liberated.

Secure in the knowledge that the government would be responsible for the girls' rehabilitation, we made a mad dash to rescue as many of the remaining Kamlaris as we could and expanded the rescue program to all five districts where the bonding custom was practiced. Between the Maghe festival in January 2010 and April of that year, the Nepal Youth Foundation liberated 4,500 girls from bondage.

The girls returned home from the demonstration in Kathmandu elated, confident that the government would heed the public outcry against the kamlari practice. But liberation was only the first step in their long journey to a normal life. Many of them were suffering from deep psychological scars as a result of abuse by their employers, the loss of their childhoods and the absence of the comforts of family life. Some were plagued by nightmares, sleep deprivation and anxiety.

To meet this challenge, therapists at the the Ankur Psychosocial Counseling Center trained more than 150 former Kamlaris as peer counselors to provide therapy and comfort to the liberated girls. Having suffered the trauma of bondage themselves, these young women understood the psychological challenges the girls faced when they returned home. The freed Kamlari participated in group therapy sessions, where they were able to speak candidly about their problems and find reassurance in the company of others who had lived through similar experiences. Peer counselors also held private sessions with the girls and visited them at home to help them overcome the conflicts and pressures arising from their reintegration into the family. The peer-counseling program alleviated the suffering of thousands of young women and helped them to make wiser choices about their future.

When they returned home, the girls had two options—they could attend school or enroll in a vocational training program. Whatever their choice, they all initially attended an intensive remedial literacy course created by the foundation to teach them to read, write and do simple math. Some were determined to go to school even though they were already teenagers and would lag far behind their classmates. After completing the bridging course, many enrolled in the local public school in 5th grade.

At first, the overcrowding in the classrooms was unbearable. The return of thousands of former Kamlaris resulted in the virtual collapse of some of the local public schools. Sometimes, more than 100 students were forced to vie for space in a single classroom, and there was a shortage of teachers. We felt responsible for the overcrowding and there was little prospect that the government would rectify the situation. With the villagers providing unskilled labor, we built more than 60 spacious new classrooms at existing government schools throughout the area and hired additional teachers. Some of the returned girls proved to be excellent students and were able to catch up to their grade level relatively quickly. Many of these young women now attend college.

But not all the Kamlaris wanted to enroll in school after the bridging classes. Early on, we realized that vocational training for these girls was critically important. A 16 or 17 year-old girl returning home after years of servitude, uneducated and illiterate, presented a serious economic burden to her family. There was intense pressure to marry her off as soon as possible to avoid the responsibility of supporting her. But if she could earn an income by working or starting her own business, the family would be relieved of the responsibility of supporting her, and she could play a role in contributing to their upkeep.

To meet this challenge, in 2012 we expanded a vocational guidance and training program to serve the freed Kamlaris. We had created the Vocational Education and Career Counseling program five years previously to address the acute needs of jobless youngsters in Kathmandu. The unemployment rate in Nepal hovers around 46 percent. Although there is a demand for employees in some fields, most young people lack the necessary skills. To prepare them for the workforce, the center has provided vocational guidance and training for hundreds of young people. The large majority have found good jobs in a variety of occupations.

A counselor from the center helps the girls explore their strengths and interests, and identify a career they would enjoy that would also lead to employment. They can choose from a wide variety of occupations, ranging from graphic designer to pig farmer. Once the students complete the course, counselors help them to find suitable jobs. Over 1,000 former Kamlaris have been trained, and the vast majority of them have found jobs as web site designers, computer programmers, motorcycle mechanics, cooks, tailors, electricians, lab technicians and more.

We were surprised that many of the liberated girls were intensely entrepreneurial and wanted to be self-employed. They preferred to run their own show. To assist these budding capitalists, we created a course to teach them the basics of small business management, entrepreneurship, marketing, accounting and other essential skills.

With the foundation's help, the girls have established 42 cooperatives so they can open savings accounts and borrow money at below-market rates. The Nepal Youth Foundation jump-started the lending program with a fund of $68,000 and members of the co-ops have supplemented this sum with monthly savings and interest income. To date, 750 girls or their families have borrowed money to start their own businesses.

Manjita is a leader of the cooperative movement. She was sold at the age of nine to an abusive employer for $30 a year. One of the most active former Kamlaris in the anti-bonding crusade, she is determined to promote economic independence for the liberated girls. Manjita is the founder of a successful cooperative. She is studying management and finance in college, and plans to start a development bank. Recently, we visited a bookstore together, and she headed right for a shelf of self-help books. Without hesitation, she picked out a book entitled, "How to Become a Millionaire." I have no doubt that Manjita will become the first Tharu J.P. Morgan.

Some of the enterprises started by the girls have been a smashing success. Many former Kamlaris are now supporting their families, paying for the education of their siblings and putting themselves through college. Their transformation from being a financial burden to contributors to their families' economic survival is changing the perception of the role of women in the local culture.

Nanu is a striking example. She spent 10 miserable years working as a Kamlari before she was rescued by the foundation. After completing the bridging class, she opened a small grocery shop and canteen with $18 of her own savings and a loan of $200. A year later, she joined a cooperative, borrowed $300 and opened a second shop. Each time she repaid a loan, she borrowed even more to expand her business. Four years later, her net worth was over $21,000, an enormous sum in Nepal. She now supports her family of seven and has grand plans to open a hotel in the future.

Our goal and our dream is to turn responsibility for the Indentured Daughters Program over to the liberated girls. It won't be long before we can do so. They are capable, passionate about the anti-bonding cause and eager to assume leadership. In 2010, 11 of the former Kamlaris started a non-governmental organization they called the Freed Kamlari Development Forum. They held elections and established branches in all five districts where the bonding custom had been practiced. We provided training in leadership, management, communication, political activism and human rights principles for the forum's leaders.

Its mission is to rescue and rehabilitate bonded girls, advocate against the kamlari custom, and, together with the counselors trained by the Ankur Psychosocial Counseling Center in Kathmandu, campaign against early marriage. Membership in the forum has swelled to more than 4,500 returned girls. Since the members are from every village and hamlet in the area, they are well aware of what is going on in the lives of the local girls, and thus perfectly positioned to prevent bonding.

At first, the girls accompanied our staff on rescue missions—surprise visits to homes that harbored a Kamlari. It didn't take long before they headed out on their own. Marching up to a house, they would knock on the door to confront the employer. Later, they used a different tactic, warning employers in advance that they were breaking the law by employing a Kamlari. During Maghe, forum members boldly took on the middlemen who dared to venture into the districts to make bonding arrangements, threatening to report them to the police. These empowered young women have become fierce advocates for freedom, defending their rights and fighting for girls who are still bonded. They are determined that their little sisters will not continue to suffer as Kamlaris.

In 2012, the Nepal Youth Foundation invited 100 of the most committed, dynamic freed Kamlari to a two-day conference; the goal of the conference was to motivate them to become even more effective champions for their cause. As speakers, we invited women members of Parliament from the three major political parties—Maoists, Congress and Unified Marxist-Leninists—and asked them not to focus on partisan politics, but rather to explain how and why they had run for office, and how to advocate effectively for a position.

They spoke passionately about their own suffering, the gender discrimination they had experienced and the reasons they had become spokeswomen for their communities. Some were from large, impoverished families and had not been allowed to go school because they were girls. One had been a bonded servant at a young age. They urged the girls to continue to work tirelessly to end the bonding custom and offered their support.

At the beginning of the meeting, each girl was asked what she wanted to do with her life. "Teacher, doctor, lawyer, journalist, social worker," they responded in turn. It was thrilling to listen to these young women, who not so long ago had worked as kitchen slaves, talk about their dreams for a fulfilling life.

The girls were deeply moved and inspired. After the conference, one of them said, "When I hear the stories of the speakers, I too remembered my past, and with tears in my eyes I built a confidence that yes, I, too, can do."

CHAPTER FOURTEEN

FREE, FREE AT LAST

On May 8, 2012, a poised young woman in her early 20s, dressed in a beautiful Tharu costume, stepped onto the stage at the Oslo Freedom Forum, an annual human rights conference. She had been invited as a guest speaker to talk about child labor and her experience as a bonded servant from the age of six. Addressing an international audience of distinguished guests gathered in the ornate hall, she joined her hands together, bowed to the audience, and began: "Namaste, and good morning. It is me—Urmila Chaudhary."

Yes, the very same Urmila we left at the end of Chapter One, after she returned to her family in Dang following almost 11 years spent in servitude. During all those years, Urmila never gave up her dream of going to school. Although several people tried to dissuade her, saying that she was too old to begin school and should instead enroll in a vocational training program, she insisted that she was going to get an education. She completed the bridging class and enrolled in the local public school in 5th grade at the age of 17, even though this meant that she had to sit in a classroom with much younger children. By the time she completed 10th grade, the end of high school in Nepal, she was 23 years old.

From the moment she returned home, Urmila was determined to fight for the freedom of the many Kamlari girls who still lived in slavery. Her extraordinary commitment to the cause was demonstrated when she joined a rally against the bonding practice even before reuniting with her family following her liberation. In the ensuing years, Urmila has been relentless in her efforts to promote the anti-bonding agenda. She has performed in street plays to raise awareness, visited families to convince them not to send their daughters away, and boarded busses at checkpoints during the Maghe festival to be sure that no bonded girls were leaving for work.

Urmila was one of the founders of the Freed Kamlari Development Forum and was elected the first president of the Dang chapter in 2012.

She was a leader of the march in Kathmandu in 2009 that resulted in the government's acceptance of financial responsibility for the education of the returned Kamlaris, and headed the delegation that met with the president, the prime minister and other government officials to promote the anti-bonding cause. Following the march, Urmila reflected, "It makes me feel wonderful to think that we, who were destined to life among dirty dishes, are now in the schools, in the offices and talking to the president and the prime minister."

By 2013, the kamlari practice had been practically eradicated. Of the 18,000 to 20,000 girls who had been sold when we began our campaign in 2000, our foundation had rescued over 13,000, and other organizations had liberated about 2,000. As a result of the awareness campaign, many parents voluntarily brought their bonded daughters home or decided not to send them away. At the time of this writing, about 300 girls are still living in bondage. We have been unable to determine their whereabouts, but the fierce girls of the Freed Kamlari Development Forum continue the search.

Tragically, there are some Kamlaris who are lost to their families altogether. One of the most appalling consequences of the bonding practice is that a substantial number of girls perished during their servitude, or simply disappeared. We estimate that since we began the eradication campaign, about 100 girls have met such a fate. In cases where girls disappeared, the parents often did not know what happened to their daughters. There was no way of knowing if their daughters had been trafficked to India, had simply lost contact with their families or had met a tragic death. Sometimes, parents were aware that their daughters had perished, but the employers' explanation of the cause of death was questionable. Because most of them are illiterate farmers, the parents did not have the means or education to probe further into the conditions that led to their daughters' deaths. They were simply forced to accept the explanations given by the employers.

In 2013, members of the forum launched a campaign to investigate the death of a 12 year-old Kamlari named Srijana Chaudhary (no relation to Urmila). Srijana worked for a powerful, well-connected family in Kathmandu. In March, her father received a telephone call from the employer informing him that his daughter was ill. He left immediately for Kathmandu. When he arrived, he was told that Srijana had committed suicide by dousing herself with kerosene and setting it alight. At the police station, he signed a document he could not read, stating that Srijana had killed herself. The family offered him 10,000 rupees—about $100—as compensation for her death. He refused the money and returned home, broken-hearted.

Outraged by the death of Srijani, members of the Freed Kamlari Development Forum asked the police to investigate. When their request was denied, they traveled to Kathmandu to conduct their own investigation. They found inconsistencies in the employer's account of Srijana's death and repeated their request for an inquiry. Once again, the police refused. In response, forum members and other anti-kamlari activists organized mass protests and strikes across South Nepal, blocking roads, forcing schools and businesses to close, and bringing life to a virtual standstill.

On June 2, the protestors, led by Urmila, staged a sit-in at the ornate iron gate of Singha Durbar, the old palace that serves as the country's main government building in Kathmandu. When their grievances were not addressed after three days, they tried to enter the restricted area surrounding the building. The police responded with force, beating the girls back. A policeman grabbed Urmila by the neck and pushed her to the ground. "This is the leader," he shouted, "hold her!" She lost consciousness and suffered internal injuries, as well as trauma to her head. When Urmila woke up in the hospital, she said that the police had beaten the girls "by stick, by boot, by hand."

The scenes of the beatings were played on national television, and there was an enormous public outcry protesting the brutality of the police and demanding the eradication of the kamlari practice. Shortly thereafter, for the first time, the government specifically pledged to end the enslavement of the Kamlaris and to rigorously enforce its edict. It also promised to free the remaining Kamlaris, prosecute the families that employed them, investigate the deaths and disappearances of Kamlaris and pay compensation to Srijana's family for the death of their daughter.

Urmila has gained international attention as an ardent and articulate activist against child slavery. She has made numerous appearances on television and at conferences, advocating for the emancipation and education of girls around the world. In October 2013, she was one of the first recipients of the Youth Courage Award bestowed by Gordon Brown, the United Nations special envoy for global education.

She plans to become a lawyer so that she can work to combat the inequities in Nepali society. I was about the same age as Urmila when I decided to go to law school at George Washington University, and for much the same reasons. It's a long way from Washington, D.C. in 1951 to the Dang District in Nepal 63 years later, but it lifts my spirits to know that the determination to carry on the fight for a just society lives on in young women like Urmila.

The culmination of the campaign against child bondage came during the Maghe festival in 2014, when the government declared January 15 Kamlari Freedom Day to mark the eradication of the practice. The occasion was celebrated in Dang with a parade, speeches and an award ceremony.

Som and I watched as hundreds of liberated girls marched in their long dresses, chanting slogans and raising their fists in the air. It took me back to the first demonstration I participated in, when there were still thousands of girls bonded away, and we were not sure if we would be able to end the selling of Tharu children. As we stood on the sidelines, a few of the girls motioned to me to join the march, and so I walked with them—for the last time.

We proceeded to an open area where the girls sat on the ground, and Som and I were ushered to a stage overflowing with local and national government officials. To me, the most important persons on the stage were Urmila, Som and Man Bahadur, all of whom received awards that day. There was an endless round of speeches by government representatives pledging their undying opposition to the kamlari practice and promising that it would never be allowed to resurface.

As I sat on the stage looking out at the sea of faces of determined, assertive former Kamlaris, I harkened back to the time I first visited

Dang 13 years earlier, almost to the day. I remembered the little orphan girl sobbing relentlessly by her uncle's side, begging not to be sent back to work for her heartless employer, and how enraged I was when I learned later that he had sold her and her sister to pay for the cost of his son's wedding.

On this day, I knew for certain that no little girl in Nepal would ever again be condemned to spending her childhood as a bonded servant. Nor would her daughter, her granddaughter, or her great-granddaughter. The flow of child slaves to the kitchens of the elite has come to an end.

Liberated girls marching on the streets of Kathmandu

Street play performed along the march

Manjita - former Kamlari, future banker

Man Bahadur Chhetri with freed Kamlari

Computer training for ex-Kamlaris

Instruction in modern farming methods

Minu started a business as a motorcycle mechanic with a loan from cooperative

Sewing training

Selling bamboo products made by business financed by cooperative

Nina at beauty parlor she started with borrowed funds

Urmila leading the charge at a rally

Reunited with her family in Dang

Urmila tutoring liberated Kamlaris at hostel for girls who cannot live at home

Here we are together in my garden

Urmila today

My last march – Kamlari Freedom Day, January 15, 2014

AFTERWORD

If I have one regret, it is that I did not discover Nepal until I was almost 60 years old. I sometimes think about how much more I could have done if I had started my work there 10 or 20 years earlier. Yet I take pride in what the Nepal Youth Foundation has been able to accomplish, and the fact that we have created an organization that will continue to serve the needs of impoverished Nepali children for years to come. The promise I made to myself on that trek 30 years ago as I lay in my sleeping bag in the dark of night—to devote my life to educating Nepali children—has been fulfilled, and even surpassed.

In June 2012, on the occasion of my 87th birthday, I announced my retirement as president of the foundation and the appointment of Som as my successor. It was a bittersweet moment. I was leaving the work to which I had devoted myself intensely for almost 30 years, but at the same time I was taking a major step toward fulfilling my most ardent wish: that NYF continue to improve the lives of Nepali children after I am gone. As the new president, Som has the skills, passion and experience to realize my dream.

Since the establishment of the foundation in June 1990, the organization has had a major impact on the lives of more than 45,000 disadvantaged children by educating them, improving their health or liberating them from slavery. More than 13,000 girls have been freed from bonded labor, at a cost of $100 each, and over 15,000 children have been restored to health at the nutrition centers, at a cost of $260 for a month of hospitalization and parental education. Thousands of other youngsters have received scholarships, shelter and medical care.

In the course of working to better the lot of children in a society so different from my own, I have learned much and grown in ways I could not have imagined 30 years ago. Every step of the way, Som and our outstanding staff in Nepal have played a pivotal role.

Early on, we resolved on a core principle—to finish what we started. We would not abandon children under our sponsorship until they could live independently, and we would apply the same principle of steadfastness to our programs. This was not an easy path to follow for a relatively small organization that depends entirely on donations.

We had seen too many non-governmental organizations provide educational support to impoverished students for a couple of years and then discontinue the scholarships, and we were determined to continue our assistance until the children in our program could stand on their own. When we undertake a child's education, we offer continuous support through high school, vocational training to those who do not go on to college, and a college education or even a graduate degree to the academically gifted. Few organizations are able or willing to undertake this responsibility on a mass basis because it involves a commitment over many years.

Sustainability is even more challenging when it comes to programs that address problems such as child slavery and malnutrition. We could not and did not want to fund the Indentured Daughters Program or the Nutritional Rehabilitation Homes in perpetuity. Our approach was to create and run these projects successfully for several years, and then convince the government to assume responsibility. We learned a hard lesson from our experience with the city of Kathmandu's takeover of the daycare center for the children of sweepers in the early '90s. It is not enough to persuade the government to adopt an existing program—we need to remain involved in the transitional, "post-handoff" period. To this day, even though the government is educating the returned Kamlaris and running eight of the 16 Nutritional Rehabilitation Homes, we continue to monitor the programs to assure that they run smoothly, offering advice and support where appropriate.

Perhaps most important of all is our conviction that the success of our undertakings depends on the buy-in, expertise, wisdom and enthusiasm of the Nepali people themselves. The country is full of smart, idealistic and committed individuals who know what programs are needed, whether they are feasible and sustainable and how to implement them. The Nepal Youth Foundation has an office in the

United States that is devoted to administration and fundraising, as well as a strong, committed board of directors, but ideas for new programs originate in Nepal and are implemented by locals. We owe our success over the years to adherence to our core principle that it is the people of Nepal themselves who know what they need to achieve a prosperous and just society and how they can best realize it.

The Nepal Youth Foundation is in the process of turning over responsibility for the Indentured Daughters Program to the strong, capable members of the Freed Kamlari Development Forum. We will continue to provide whatever help is necessary to assure that there is not a single bonded child left in Nepal, and that the liberated girls get the training they need to earn a decent livelihood. Vocational training is expensive and requires expertise, so we will maintain our involvement with this aspect of the program. And, of course, we will continue our scholarship program, as well as operate the eight remaining satellite nutritional centers until 2018, by which time the government will assume responsibility.

The Kathmandu facility, however, will remain under our management so that it can continue to serve as a center for nutrition education and rehabilitation. As we have learned, the appalling prevalence of malnutrition is due to the lack of knowledge rather than poverty, and there is still a dire need for information about what constitutes a healthy diet.

The foundation recently started a pilot program to combine first-rate preschool education with training in nutrition. There is ample evidence that malnutrition has long-term implications for a child's physical and cognitive development, and that the earlier children begin to benefit from nutritional interventions, the better the outcome. We have established eight early-childhood education classrooms at public schools in the Kathmandu area and in a rural district, and trained the teachers in the principles of nutrition, as well as preschool education. The teachers in turn train the mothers of the 20 children in each class in good nutritional practices and encourage them to share their knowledge with their neighbors. Our hope is that these mothers will form the nucleus of a movement that will spread information about proper nutrition in rural areas of the country. Each classroom has an attached kitchen, and the children will receive a healthy midday meal made with inexpensive local ingredients, which will be prepared by the mothers whenever feasible.

If these eight centers prove to be successful, we will expand the preschool program to other areas. Ultimately, we hope to convince the government to take ~~take~~ it over and establish similar classes at the 30,000 public primary schools in the country.

A project that is especially close to my heart is the construction of Olgapuri Village—"Olga's Little Oasis." For more than 20 years, the children at J and K Houses have lived in rented buildings designed for private residential use. As housing in the Kathmandu Valley has grown more and more expensive and the cost of land has skyrocketed, we have been compelled to move the children from one unsuitable house to another, with ever-dwindling space for these healthy, active kids to play outdoors. Our dream to build a permanent, safe, attractive home seemed a distant fantasy.

But with the help of generous donors, including a family foundation, our board members and others, we purchased three acres of beautiful farmland not far from the city, and are in the process of building homes for the children. The houses will accommodate the children of J and K House through high school, and there will be ample recreational facilities: a basketball court, table tennis, badminton, playgrounds, a library and a performance hall. We will have a small working farm to provide vegetables and fresh milk to the children at the houses and our other programs in the Kathmandu area. J and K House kids will work at the farm on weekends, getting their hands dirty and learning useful skills.

There is enough land so that we can realize another long-held dream of establishing our own vocational training facility. In a country where the unemployment rate is 46 percent, but there are jobs available for skilled workers, we plan to provide first-class vocational training for 300 youngsters a year, tailored specifically to the needs of the job market.

For me, the most thrilling aspect of Olgapuri Village is that the J and K House children will finally have a place they can call their own. The houses were established in the early '90s, and the current batch of kids is the second generation to grow up there. The first-generation youngsters come back to visit, bringing their spouses and children to show them where they spent their childhoods—and always to a different house than the one in which they grew up. From now on, and for many years to come, children who grow up at the homes will be able to show their own children the place where they were raised with love and care until they reached adulthood.

We hope that Olgapuri Village will help bring alumni together and inspire them to become involved with the younger generation by acting as mentors. One day, perhaps, we can turn management of the houses over to the young men and women who spent their childhoods there.

In a conjunction of events that means a great deal to me, the Village will be completed in 2015, the year that marks the 25th anniversary of the founding of the Nepal Youth Foundation, my 90th birthday and the publication of this book.

As for my personal odyssey, nothing I have ever done compares to the satisfaction and joy of the last 30 years. In a world beset by mass shootings, selfishness and greed, my time with these children has sustained my faith in humanity. To witness their evolution from sad, frightened, frail little beings into happy and loving adults, solid citizens and good parents, and to have had a part in that evolution, gives me more happiness than I have words to describe.

And there is something else—young Nepali children, especially girls, can be exuberantly loving in word and deed. The affection lavished on me by the children when they are little, especially the K House girls, is sometimes ridiculously extravagant. This fervent adoration diminishes as their teen years approach and they wise up, but while it lasts, I lurch between shameless basking in the love and toe-cringing embarrassment at its expression.

I am not particularly introspective by nature, but once in a while, before I fall asleep, I think about my long journey from Transylvania to Kathmandu. I remember my father and his audacious decision to leave Europe to seek a better life for our family, and my mother sitting at the kitchen table, listening with compassion to so many woeful stories. I think back to my desperate longing for a wider world as a youngster, and my travels around the country in search of what I wanted to do with my life. I recall my career as a lawyer, my marriage to Judd and our years of love and struggle and my beloved siblings and stepsons. And then I think of my first trip to Nepal and the astounding, unexpected discovery of what would become my life's work—and the intense joy and sense of fulfillment resulting from that insight. As I nod off to sleep, I think to myself, "How lucky can an old lady get?"

POSTSCRIPT
Written Ten Days After the Devastating Earthquake in Nepal

At noon on April 25, 2015, a massive earthquake devastated the lands and people of Nepal. The death toll is expected to exceed 10,000, with many crushed under the rubble of archaic and poorly-built houses. Much of the country's rich architectural heritage—ancient temples and revered monasteries—has been reduced to rubble.

I was in my office at home in Kathmandu with a foundation employee when the shaking started. We both fell to the floor with the first sharp bolt and rolled around for what seemed like a long time. He grabbed my arm and kept reassuring me, "It's ok, Olga didi, (a Nepali word that means "older sister"), it's ok." The irony is that I am a California girl and knew what was going on, whereas he, like almost everyone else in Nepal, had never experienced a substantial earthquake before. A heater on wheels with a tank of propane gas in the back rolled toward us. I shoved it back with my feet and tried to shimmy under my desk, my "go to" place in the event of a quake.

The shaking stopped after about a minute, and like millions of others, we went outside for safety. I sat in the garden with several employees and my anxious dogs for a few hours, until the most terrifying aftershocks subsided. Beyond the high brick wall of my garden is an open area that was soon filled with frightened Nepalis. Each time an aftershock shook the ground, a great cry would rise up from the crowd. It was strangely comforting, because it gave voice to how we were all feeling. As a reserved Westerner, my only outward reaction was to look scared as I sat in a bamboo chair waiting for the next tremor.

For the next five days, most of the population of the affected areas across Nepal slept outdoors. Every open space in congested Kathmandu was filled with petrified people, too afraid to enter their houses, if their homes were still standing at all. Shortly after the major aftershocks stopped, people started to arrive at my house to take refuge in my large garden. The crowd ultimately reached 50 people. Among them were two babies, one five days old and the other a month old, their parents, and sundry friends of friends I'd never met.

My guests included 20 former Kamlari girls who had come from West Nepal to perform their beautiful dances at my 90th birthday party. It was scheduled for 4 pm on April 25th, four hours after the earthquake struck. Som, his wife Sajani and the staff at the foundation office in Nepal, had arranged an elaborate weekend of celebrations. Six hundred people were invited, and for weeks, the J and K House children had been rehearsing dances and songs they had composed for the party.

The Kamlari were not together when the earthquake hit, but scattered in different areas of Kathmandu. A few witnessed terrible devastation and saw people buried under the rubble of old temples. We managed to gather them into a group and they arrived in my garden, traumatized and fearful. The girls dusted off a large tarp we found in a shed, spread it out on the lawn and fell asleep in the sun, exhausted.

When they awakened, they went to work helping to prepare lunch for the 50 people present—chopping vegetables, cooking lentils, and dishing up the biggest pot of rice I have ever seen. I thought my dining table would collapse under the weight. As they sat outdoors chopping broccoli, cauliflower, potatoes, ginger and garlic, they gossiped and laughed together, and some of the tension began to evaporate.

Even as the aftershocks continued, they talked about where they were at the time of the quake and the relief they felt that their families were safe because their home districts in West Nepal were not affected. I told them about my own experiences with earthquakes in the States: that I was quite accustomed to waking up a few times a year with my bed shaking due to earth tremors. When this happened, I just pulled the covers over my head, turned over and went back to sleep. Unlike most Nepalis, I said, I intended to continue to sleep in my comfy bed rather than under the open sky. I am a California girl, after all.

That night, my guests went to sleep outdoors on mats under a tarp. Tremors continued throughout the night. When it began to rain, they ran inside for shelter. The next morning, one girl told me that when the tremors started they woke up, frightened. She reminded the others about what I had said about going back to sleep if I was awakened by a tremor, so they took my advice and did the same.

As we sat outside in the sun the next morning, a girl named Reeta came to sit beside me on the bamboo sofa. She told me in her halting English that she had wanted to meet me for years to thank the foundation for liberating her from bondage and sending her to school. She was sold at the age of nine and worked for several years for an abusive employer. Today, she is in college and leads one of the 42 cooperatives the liberated girls created to provide business loans to former Kamlaris. I felt embarrassed that this young woman, who had come so far to provide entertainment at my birthday party, and who had suffered so much stress and anxiety as a result, thought it necessary to thank me for her liberation years ago.

Urmila was among my guests. She was everywhere, helping everyone. Whether it was setting up the tarps, taking care of the children, or leading the vegetable-chopping brigade, there seemed to be nothing she was unwilling or unable to do to help the crowd stay comfortable and well-fed. I had noticed her leadership qualities before, but those days in my garden deepened my affection and admiration for her.

After a couple of days, the former Kamlari were able to make the 14-hour bus journey home, and my house gradually emptied. When I assessed the damage, I discovered that there were several severe cracks in one of the walls upstairs that rendered the upper floor uninhabitable, but the downstairs, where my bedroom is located, was largely unharmed.

I was relieved to learn that the J and K House children and our Nepali staff and their families were all safe. We had supplies stored in a shed at J House for just such an emergency, with sleeping bags, tents, blankets, tarps, water and other items. The kids camped in a field outside the house in large tents. The smaller boys seemed to enjoy the experience, asking me eagerly when we would be having another earthquake. Many of the young adults who grew up at the Houses came streaming back. J and K Houses are their real homes, and everyone wants to be with family when they feel vulnerable and scared. They were a big help to the aunties and uncle who supervise the homes, running after the little boys in the open field and helping with the cooking. After four or five days, the children moved back indoors, like much of the rest of the population.

I had purchased my return ticket to California months before and was due to leave on the night of April 29, four days after the earthquake. A few hours before my departure, I stopped at J and K House to say my farewells. My last day with the kids is always difficult for me, but this time the children cheered me up by performing the songs and dances they had intended to present at my birthday party. Among them was a dance they composed to accompany "Resham Firiri,"my favorite Nepali tune. The older kids sang "We Are the World" in chorus.

The chaos of the Kathmandu airport was even more outrageous than usual. Emergency provisions were arriving, and many foreigners stood by for flights, trying to escape.

I arrived back in San Francisco the next day, a bit smelly, since I hadn't had a shower in a week. Water was in short supply, and ran out altogether at my house the day I left. My departure was even more distressing than usual because I was leaving at a time when the country was in such a ruinous state. I considered staying on, but decided that I would just be using up precious resources in the aftermath of the quake, and I could make more of an impact by returning to the States to raise funds for the relief effort. Sure enough, the day after I left, my house was put to good use as a storage and packing facility for relief supplies; the lower floor is jammed with tarps and huge boxes of rice, lentils and water filters. I know that Som and our competent and committed staff will do a stellar job of providing aid where it's most needed, if they have the funds to do so.

The devastation caused by the earthquake (7.9 on the Richter scale), is unimaginable. As of this writing, it is estimated that more than 17,000 people have been injured, many of them seriously. Half a million houses have been razed to the ground. Whole villages close to the epicenter of the quake, in the Gorkha and Sindhupalchok Districts, west of Kathmandu, were completely destroyed—not a single house was left standing. The earthquake triggered an avalanche on Mount Everest that killed at least 18 people, making April 25, 2015 the deadliest day in memory on the mountain.

After the worst tremors died down and we were sure that the J and K House children, our employees and their families were safe, we began to plan relief efforts. Som called a meeting of the foundation's senior employees at my house. We decided to focus our energies in three stages: short-term for immediate relief, medium-term for efforts that would continue a few weeks after the earthquake, and long-term relief to help rebuild the country.

The most urgent need was for shelter and medical care. Som spoke with the senior doctors at the main hospitals, who desperately needed medical and surgical supplies for the many hundreds of injured people waiting for operations. He authorized them to purchase $40,000 worth of these items in the local market at our expense. One hospital was in acute need of a portable x-ray machine called a C-Arm, which could quickly and accurately diagnose injuries. There were none available in Nepal, but we found one in Calcutta at a cost of $28,000. We paid for it and the machine was delivered a few days later.

The government hospitals in the Kathmandu Valley ran out of beds almost immediately after the earthquake hit and many injured patients were sleeping in the corridors or outside in the open air. We bought 200 mattresses and bedding and delivered them to the hospitals within 24 hours.

Most importantly, the hospitals were desperate to discharge patients who were ready to go home, but could not leave because their houses had been destroyed or their relatives could not come for them. To relieve the pressure on the hospitals, we turned two of our Nutritional Rehabilitation Homes, in Kathmandu and Pokhara, into transitional shelters for these patients. They are ideal for this purpose — safe and clean, and our trained staff can provide a nutritious diet, as well as some basic medical care. The J House alumni are serving as volunteers at the shelter, as are 40 former Kamlaris training to become medical assistants.

Sajani, Som's wife, arranged for busloads of new mothers and their babies to travel from the government maternity hospital in Kathmandu to their homes. The hospital was badly damaged in the earthquake and women were giving birth as they lay on the floor in the corridors. Many others waited hours for care. Mothers and newborns who could not go home but were ready for discharge, found refuge at the Kathmandu nutritional center transitional shelter.

A few days after the earthquake, Som and Man Bahadur drove two huge trucks loaded with tarps and food supplies to an area in the Dhading District that had been severely affected by the quake. Aside from a helicopter drop of 35 bags of rice a couple of days earlier, the area had received no assistance. The foundation's staff delivered supplies to other areas that had been badly hit, such as the Kavre District.

We purchased 1,000 tarps from a local manufacturer to shelter families, and 50 school tents that will accommodate 1,500 children so that classes can resume as soon as possible. These will be delivered in two weeks.

Within 10 days of the earthquake, we had reached 1,847 families and provided assistance to 13,000 people. By that time, international aid began pouring into the country, so the initial phase of our efforts was largely over, except for the continued operation of the Nutritional Rehabilitation Home transitional shelters and the daycare center described below.

Olgapuri Village is located close to Bungamati, an ancient woodcarver's village where almost all the houses were old, shoddily constructed brick structures. The village was virtually flattened in the earthquake. We have an affiliation with a school near Bungamati, which mercifully survived the quake. After we had it inspected for safety, we opened a daycare center there. Our goal is to enable the traumatized children of the village to spend their days in a secure and happy place while their parents rebuild their lives.

Volunteer teachers from a private school in Kathmandu are in charge of instruction, and there is a lot of singing, dancing and drawing. Counselors from the Ankur Psychosocial Counseling Center are on hand to offer help and comfort. The volunteer kitchen staff is astounded at how much these children eat—they cook double the usual amounts, and even that seems to be insufficient. The shelter also harbors a little heroine: a 10 year-old girl who saved the lives of her one and two-year old sisters when their house collapsed. We are in the process of opening more daycare centers in the Kathmandu Valley.

One serious issue in the recovery effort is the approaching monsoon season. Monsoon in Nepal is otherworldly. Torrential rain hammers the country for weeks on end. This will lead to severe mudslides, or worse, the spread of infectious diseases. We are working with the School of Engineering at Kathmandu University, the best institute of higher education in the country, to meet this challenge. They are designing inexpensive, rain-proof shelters, which our foundation plans to distribute to as many people in need as we can afford.

Our long-term post-earthquake plan is two-fold—to train Nepalis for employment in the building trades, and to facilitate the reconstruction of some of the hundreds of thousands of homes and schools that have been destroyed. It is estimated that 500,000 houses and 24,000 schoolrooms have collapsed, leaving one million children without access to education. There is no way these schools can be rebuilt until next winter, following the end of the monsoon. The School of Engineering at Kathmandu University has designed lightweight, low cost, prefabricated sustainable housing and will provide free training in construction to homeowners so they can rebuild with these materials. These skills can also be used to reconstruct classrooms. The foundation will supply the funds to purchase building materials for homes and classrooms.

Training provided to homeowners by Kathmandu University, as well as additional programs we will conduct to teach construction skills, will help reduce the staggering 46 percent unemployment rate in the country. For the foreseeable future, competent construction workers will be in great demand.

This program, which we call "Rebuild," will speed the return to normalcy for Nepal's children, back into safe homes and safe schools. There is endless potential to expand the program.

A 7.9 earthquake would present a challenge anywhere in the world. But in an impoverished country like Nepal, where much of the population lived on the brink of economic disaster even before its heritage and infrastructure were laid to waste, it is a calamity.

Nevertheless, two things give me hope. First is the extraordinary resilience of the Nepali people, their collaborative spirit and their strong family ties. These will help to heal the psychological wounds left by the disaster and unite them in rebuilding their country. The second is the overwhelming outpouring of sympathy and aid from the international community. The Nepal Youth Foundation received more donations in a shorter period of time for earthquake relief than we have for any cause at any other time in our 25-year history. Our hard-working, creative, committed staff in Nepal will make sure that these funds are put to the best possible use, swiftly and efficiently. Today, 10 days after disaster struck, I am still filled with sorrow for the suffering of the Nepali people, but I look forward to helping, through the work of our foundation, to rebuild and restore a country I have grown to love.

One of many old buildings in Kathmandu
devastated by the earthquake

Sheltering among the ruins

Waiting for help in a crude shed

J and K House kids camping outdoors following quake

Farewell dance by J and K House kids intended to
be performed at my birthday party

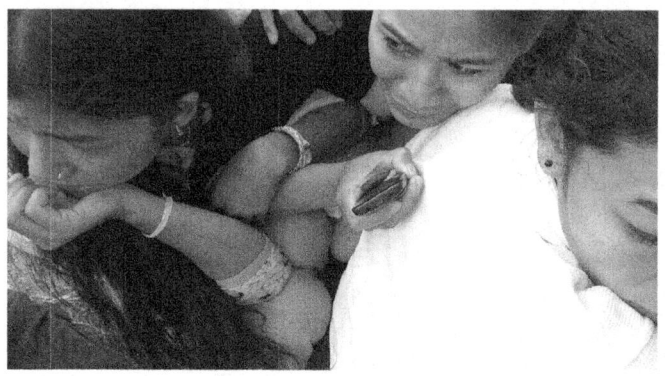

Former kamlaris stressed after earthquake

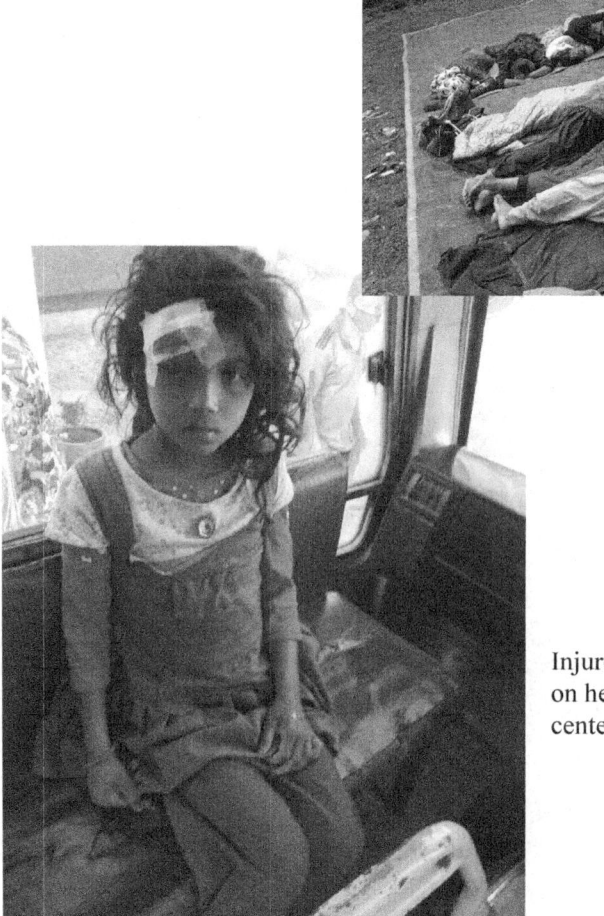

Resting at last in my garden

Injured and traumatized child on her way to the nutrition center transitional facility

Som gives tarp to elderly man whose house was destroyed

Lining up in their shattered village for distribution of rice

Patients sleeping on floor at Patan Hospital

Day care center for children who
lost homes in earthquake

School in a tent replaces
classroom that
was destroyed

The day after I left Nepal, my house became a storage
and packing facility for relief supplies

ACKNOWLEDGMENTS

Many people around the globe have contributed to the creation of this book, offering encouragement, advice and suggestions. Their common message was, "Olga, you're in your late 80s. It's time to write a book about how the Nepal Youth Foundation started and how it evolved into what it is today." Somewhat reluctantly, with Mary's help, I began. The process led me to dig deep to unearth memories of my childhood, of the many people I loved and those who helped me in my struggles over the years, and how, against all odds, I ended up in such a happy place at the age of 90.

We are extremely grateful to Victoria deGoff and Steve Sherman, as well as to Ann and Dougal Crowe, who encouraged us to write this book and financed its publication.

Many thanks to Zara Houshmand, Amanda Tong, Suzannah Lessard, Deb Carlen and Carolyn Miller, who edited various versions of the manuscript and offered valuable advice.

A host of friends and relatives looked over multiple drafts and made helpful suggestions for improvement. Thanks to Joan Anway, Max Callender, Molly Callender, Edith Freeman, Mike Gill, Jackie Kudler, Martha Molnar, Ellen Wright Montgomery, Nancy Rhodes, Mary Robinson, Julieclaire Sheppard and Haydi Sowerwine.

We are very lucky to have had Todd Towner on our team. He is a gifted, creative graphic designer who worked tirelessly and enthusiastically to produce this book. No matter what we asked, his response was always, "Sure, I can do that."

Carrie Leroy and Greg Norman of Skadden, Arps, Slate, Meagher and Flom LLP, provided legal advice pro bono.

Our thanks go out to the able and committed staff of the Nepal Youth Foundation in Nepal for their role as fact-checkers extraordinaire. They made sure that all the information about the programs and stories in this book is accurate. Their hard work and devotion to the cause of improving the lives of children in Nepal have been crucial to our success.

The Board of Directors has championed the writing of this book and has provided extraordinarily capable guidance and support to the foundation's work for more than two decades.

Lisa Cosby and Jackie Frost, our efficient and dedicated staff at the foundation's Sausalito office, are the backbone of our operations. They make sure that the office runs smoothly and that donors and others are kept up to date. We are thankful to them for their hard work.

We are hugely appreciative for the help provided by the Nepal Youth Foundation chapters in the United Kingdom, Hong Kong, Australia, and most recently, Germany. They have raised funds to sustain our programs and increased awareness about our projects around the world. Their wholehearted devotion to improving the health of Nepali children and providing them with an education has been a key factor in our success.

None of the good works set out in this book—the restoration of 15,000 malnourished children to health and the training of their mothers, the release of 13,000 girls from labor bondage, the eradication of the kamlari practice and the education of tens of thousands of very poor children—would have been possible without two components:

First, we are so grateful for the loyalty and generosity of our foundation's donors. For 25 years, they have supported us not only financially, but with encouragement and advice. They have raised funds by baking cookies, reading books and washing cars, and opened their pocketbooks, as well as their hearts to the foundation's mission. We could not ask for more caring and constructive allies.

Second, the unwavering support of Som Paneru has been invaluable in creating and administering the foundation's programs. His energy and vision have made the Nepal Youth Foundation what it is today. It is unfathomable how a farm boy who grew up a two-day walk from the nearest road in the Gorkha District of Nepal has evolved into such a capable manager. (Or for that matter how he could form such a productive and congenial partnership with an American woman twice his age.) He thinks big and has ambitious, ingenious ideas to widen the reach of the foundation's programs. His wife, Sajani, is an equally committed social worker and has helped us from the beginning by raising funds, finding jobs for our graduates, and in many other ways.

OM – This book would not have seen the light of day without the patient, able help of my partner in crime, Mary Callender. Although I suspect that she was frustrated at times with my lack of productivity, and we had numerous differences about style and substance, we did not exchange a single harsh word over the three years it took to write the book. I will always be grateful to her for her forbearance, good cheer and steadfast support.

MSC – A very special thank you from both of us to our dear friend Marybeth Bond, who introduced me to Olga in Sausalito many years ago. Marybeth invited me to travel to Nepal, where we stayed with Olga in Kathmandu, visited the foundation's programs and spent time with the children at J and K Houses. For the past three years, while we were writing this book, Marybeth has provided practical advice, boundless encouragement and an ever-present smile.

To Olga, thank you for your friendship and the trust you placed in me by letting me work with you to tell your story. You are a shining example of how one person truly can make a difference in the world. Our collaboration has given me a glimpse into what it takes to accomplish this: a combination of love and respect for people, a deep concern for social justice and a down-to-earth, "let's get it done" approach, combined with the vision to see the big picture.

I've been blessed with a large, loving supportive family including Alec Callender, Mike Durkin, Alice Stratton, Patrick Durkin, Molly Callender, Neel Keller, Chris Durkin, Sylvia Robb Malone and Elsa Sinclair, as well as 12 amazing grandchildren who have brought so much joy into my life. And finally, I am so grateful to Steve Callender, my husband, partner and best friend. You've held my hand every step of the way and I am so thankful for your love, encouragement and endless patience.

Disclaimer by Olga: Events and conversations in this book are recounted from my personal recollections, some of them stretching back more than 80 years. Though I've been blessed with a pretty good memory, specific details tend to blur over the years. I have tried to present the events described as accurately as possible, but if there are mistakes and omissions, I apologize and take full responsibility.

The stories about the Nepali children in this book are true. Their names have been changed to protect their privacy, with the exception of Urmila, Manjita and Srijana Chaudhary. The name Nepal Youth Foundation has been used throughout for clarity. However, as required by the laws of Nepal, our programs were carried out by the foundation's implementing arm in Nepal, with the financial support and supervision of the Nepal Youth Foundation.

JOIN THE NEPAL YOUTH FOUNDATION FAMILY

If you've been inspired by the stories in this book, please join us by supporting the Nepal Youth Foundation's programs. Our organization values every donation we receive, no matter the size, and we utilize your donations as efficiently as possible. For the eighth consecutive year, Charity Navigator, America's largest independent evaluator of charities, has awarded the Nepal Youth Foundation its highest rating of four stars for financial accountability and transparency. We are particularly honored because less than one percent of charities earn eight consecutive four-star ratings through this evaluation process. For more information, visit www.charitynavigator.org.

To keep in touch with the foundation online, visit our website at www.nepalyouthfoundation.org. You can "friend" us on Facebook, check out our videos on YouTube and follow our posts on Twitter. For other ways to get involved. here is a link to our website: http://www.nepalyouthfoundation.org/get-involved/creative-ways-to-support-impoverished-children/

If you would like to receive periodic email newsletters with the latest news about NYF's projects and the children we support, please sign up by emailing us at: info@nepalyouthfoundation.org.

For more information, contact us at:
Nepal Youth Foundation
3030 Bridgeway, Suite 202
Sausalito, CA 94965, USA
Telephone: (415) 331-8585

ABOUT THE AUTHORS

OLGA MURRAY was born in Transylvania in 1925 and came to the United States at the age of six with her parents and three siblings. She grew up in New York City. After graduating from Columbia University and George Washington University Law School, she worked as a research attorney at the California Supreme Court for 37 years. In 1984, approaching the age of 60, she traveled to Nepal for the first time and fell in love with the country and its people. Recognizing a critical need to improve the lot of Nepali children, she founded the Nepal Youth Foundation in 1990. Over the past 25 years, the foundation has provided education, shelter, health care and other essential services to over 45,000 Nepali children. Since 2000, more than 13,000 girls have been liberated from indentured servitude and the practice of bonding them has been eradicated. Olga divides her time between Kathmandu, Nepal, and Sausalito, California.

MARY SUTRO CALLENDER grew up in San Francisco and attended Stanford University. For many years, she wrote a weekly column entitled "Nature's Kitchen" for United Feature Syndicate that was published in newspapers throughout the United States. She had a career in philanthropy as the Executive Director of the Gamble and Michelson Foundations, and as a senior Program Officer for the Bothin, Kimball, MacDonnell and Roberts Foundations, all located in the San Francisco Bay Area. She has been an advisor to numerous nonprofit organizations, including KIPP Bay Area Schools, Food Runners and Wildlife Associates. Mary and her husband, Steve, live in Marin County, California, and they travel extensively, often to visit their 12 grandchildren.

Additional copies of this book may be purchased at

www.**olgaspromise**.org

Made in the USA
Las Vegas, NV
20 November 2022